AF829254

Strategic Leadership and Systems Thinking

This book is about a new strategic leader – one who, inspired by General Systems Theory (GST), envisions an organization in which people and groups work together interdependently across organizational divides to reach a shared, rewarding future. GST has dramatically influenced physics, biology, economics, healthcare and environmental science, but has not as yet had any significant influence on the way companies work and are structured. This new, systems way of working promises a break from the influence of Sir Isaac Newton and René Descartes – thinking that has dominated worldviews for almost 400 years – and offers workers the opportunity to find greater purpose and meaning in their work.

This book is also about leadership that recognizes the potential of enhanced organizational performance that results from the movement of the organization as system, to a new desired destination. Engaging and empowering employees, the leader unleashes their unique talents and energy and uses the previously unrecognized power of strategy processes to bridge functional silos.

Offering the latest knowledge on strategic leadership, *Strategic Leadership and Systems Thinking* will be of interest to researchers, academics, practitioners and students in the fields of leadership and organizational studies.

Peter S. DeLisi is President of Organizational Synergies and former Academic Dean of the Information Technology Leadership Program at Santa Clara University, USA.

Routledge Studies in Leadership Research

Leading in the Age of Innovations
Change of Values and Approaches
Lenka Theodoulides, Gabriela Kormancová, and David Cole

Critical Perspectives on Leadership
The Language of Corporate Power
Mark Learmonth and Kevin Morrell

Cognitive Automation and Organizational Psychology
Priming Goals as a New Source of Competitive Advantage
Alexander. D. Stajkovic and Kayla Sergent

Women's Leadership Development
Caring Environments and Paths to Transformation
Gelaye Debebe

Strategic Leadership and Systems Thinking
Peter S. DeLisi

Leadership, Gender and Ethics
Embodied Reason in Challenging Masculinities
David Knights

Digital Supply Chain Management
Reshaping Talent and Organizations
David B. Kurz and Muragan Anandarajan

Researching Leadership-As-Practice
The Reappearing Act of Leadership
Vasilisa Takoeva

For more information about this series please visit: https://www.routledge.com/Routledge-Studies-in-Leadership-Research/book-series/RSLR

Strategic Leadership and Systems Thinking

Peter S. DeLisi

Routledge
Taylor & Francis Group
NEW YORK AND LONDON

First published 2021
by Routledge
52 Vanderbilt Avenue, New York, NY 10017

and by Routledge
2 Park Square, Milton Park, Abingdon, Oxon OX14 4RN

Routledge is an imprint of the Taylor & Francis Group, an informa business

© 2021 Peter S. DeLisi

The right of Peter S. DeLisi to be identified as author of this work has been asserted by him in accordance with sections 77 and 78 of the Copyright, Designs and Patents Act 1988.

All rights reserved. No part of this book may be reprinted or reproduced or utilised in any form or by any electronic, mechanical, or other means, now known or hereafter invented, including photocopying and recording, or in any information storage or retrieval system, without permission in writing from the publishers.

Trademark notice: Product or corporate names may be trademarks or registered trademarks, and are used only for identification and explanation without intent to infringe.

Library of Congress Cataloging-in-Publication Data
Names: DeLisi, Peter S., 1937– author.
Title: Strategic leadership and systems thinking / Peter S. DeLisi.
Description: 1 Edition. | New York : Routledge, 2021. |
Series: Routledge studies in leadership research |
Includes bibliographical references andindex.
Identifiers: LCCN 2020037314 (print) | LCCN 2020037315 (ebook) |
ISBN 9780367567231 (hardback) | ISBN 9781003099154 (ebook)
Subjects: LCSH: Leadership. | System theory. | Employee motivation. |
Organizational effectiveness. | Organizational change.
Classification: LCC HD57.7 .D4724 2021 (print) |
LCC HD57.7 (ebook) | DDC658.4/092–dc23
LC record available at https://lccn.loc.gov/2020037314
LC ebook record available at https://lccn.loc.gov/2020037315

ISBN: 978-0-367-56723-1 (hbk)
ISBN: 978-0-367-56727-9 (pbk)
ISBN: 978-1-003-09915-4 (ebk)

DOI: 10.4324/9781003099154

Typeset in Sabon
by Newgen Publishing UK

To my loving wife, Cece, who did more than she could ever realize to help me with this book. A number of times during the writing of the book, I ran into serious, mental "roadblocks" and just needed someone to talk to. Sitting patiently, she would listen to my discourse and not say a word, but somehow the solution would always magically appear right after our brief encounter.

And to my daughters, Lisa and Nicole, whose kind, loving words of encouragement and support have always made me feel like a superhero.

To my brother-in-law, Leo, a 95-year-old World War II veteran, who early in my career, counseled me to accept an offer from IBM. Later, he was always there with his kind advice and support.

Contents

Figures

Tables

Acknowledgments

I met Barry Posner shortly after leaving Digital Equipment Corporation (DEC) and starting my own consulting business. At the time, I was looking for the possibility of a part-time academic role to supplement my consulting. Believing that my marketing background would contribute to the university, Barry hired me into a position in the Executive Development Center. Later, Barry left the Center and became the Business School Dean. He has since gone on to become one of the top leadership authors in the world. Through the years I have known Barry, he has been incredibly supportive and taught me much about leadership and life in an academic institution. Recently, I called on him to help me with my book publishing efforts, and once again, he was extremely supportive. He put me in contact with the editor of a major publishing company, and when that failed, encouraged me to continue my search for a publisher.

Ed Schein has been my mentor and friend over the past 30 years. I met him originally while at DEC, and hired him to consult on a number of projects. I fell in love with his work on organizational culture and leadership. That knowledge has served me extremely well over the years. He has encouraged me to write this book and even reviewed my first draft. It would take another book to describe all the things he has taught me and done for me. Thankfully, he now lives close by and I can still reach him for advice.

George Papa is a former client and friend. I met him originally while working on a consulting contract in Sacramento, California. I ended up working with George on his sales strategy, and subsequently, consulted with him at two other companies that he joined. George was a thought leader and I enjoyed exchanging creative ideas with him. He was also the best strategic sales executive I had ever met – able to think both short-term and long-term about his business.

Gubby Barlow was a healthcare executive and a client of mine. When I decided to leave DEC, I had a consulting project pending with Gubby that I thought I would have to relinquish. I will never forget Gubby's kindness when he asked me to stay on, and said, "I hired *you* to do this project, not DEC." It was such a morale booster for me, as I was just starting my own consulting company. Subsequently, Gubby moved on and hired me at two other companies and had by now become CEO of a major healthcare company.

The other clients that I wish to acknowledge are Scott Simplot and Ray Sasso, from the J.R. Simplot Company. Scott is now the CEO of the company;

Ray is now retired and the former CIO of the company. The J.R. Simplot consulting engagement was my first large-scale effort with a major corporation. It took a great leap of faith and trust on their part to hire someone with little previous consulting experience. I learned to love the people and the culture at Simplot and learned so much from that experience that I carry forward to this day.

There are many others I could mention that have contributed to this book directly, or indirectly. Tammy Madsen, a strategy professor at Santa Clara University, reviewed critical chapters of my book and gave me excellent advice about improving them. Tony Tasca, a personal friend, esteemed consultant, writer and culinary expert, also commented on several chapters of my book and helped me make some critical changes to them.

Introduction

This book is about a new kind of strategic leader – one who, inspired by systems thinking, enables a new, interdependent way of working. The latter is a departure from the machine model that focused on the parts and believed corporate performance depended upon their success. This book is also about the organization as system, a model that has been written about in theory by some, but seldom observed in practice. In this model, the members of the organization identify with, and work for, the greater good of the "whole."

When we look at the history of the industrial enterprise, the structure of organizations has been strongly influenced by the almost 400-year-old thinking of Sir Isaac Newton and René Descartes. This worldview led to the machine model of organizations. Since the end of World War II, "new age thinking" has arisen, driven by the belief that machine age thinking was not best able to deal with our complex, rapidly changing times.

One of the new organizational theories that has gained prominence is General Systems Theory (GST).[1] This will be the special focus of my book. Spurred on by physics discoveries in the early 1900s, General Systems Theory has had a profound impact on many disciplines. Some of these disciplines include physics, environmental science, biology, psychology, medicine and economics. While several authors have also used systems thinking and described its impact on organizations, little has really changed as a result. Organizations largely continue to work and to be structured along the lines of the traditional, Newtonian, machine model. They have not taken the benefits that systems thinking provides and incorporated them into modern-day organizations. Their emphasis continues to be on the individual parts of the system, rather than on their dynamic interactions.

Systems occur naturally in the outside world, but do not occur naturally in corporations. In corporations, a systems way of working needs to be enabled. To accomplish this, they need leadership that supports a culture that is participative, empowered and open. And more importantly, the organization as system needs to have processes that bring the people and groups together to work interdependently for the good of the whole enterprise. *To accomplish the latter, I am proposing strategy processes that have been the core of my strategy consulting practice for the past 30 years.*

The strategy processes that I am proposing to enable a new systems way of working are the strategy creation process and the strategy execution process. The strategy creation process brings the people together to create the desired future destination for the "whole." The strategy execution process lays out how the people will work together interdependently to move the organization to the desired future state.

Some contemporary organizations have adopted new thinking, which contains elements of systems theory, such as collaborative work and empowerment. Again, despite this new thinking, organizations continue to be siloed as they have in the past. *Despite almost universal criticism of this latter way of working, the reality is that silos persist in some form in almost all organizations.*

Why is the siloed organization so prejudicial to corporate success? Later we will discuss the roots that continue to strongly hold the siloed organization in place. It is important now to mention, however, the heightened danger of this form of working in our present times. Companies are no longer staffed by lifelong employees. The erosion of employee and employer loyalty greatly worsens the silo problem. It was difficult before for employees to identify with the organizational "whole;" now, it is almost impossible. "If I am only going to be here for a few years, does it matter if I identify with the role that my functional group plays in the success of the overall corporation?" Given this scenario, there arises a strong need for something that binds the employees together effectively in support of the corporation as a "whole."

In this book, I will focus on the new leadership role and the benefits of the organization as system. While this book does not focus on the HR issues, I believe the solution I will propose has the potential to bound individuals and groups together in serving a purpose greater than themselves. The Positive Psychologist, Martin Seligman, in his book, *Flourish*, says, "Human beings, ineluctably, want the 'meaningful life'; belonging to and serving something that you believe is bigger than you are."[2]

This nobility of purpose is sometimes highlighted by a simple, popular anecdote. It is one in which an individual observes several bricklayers and asks them what they are doing. Asking the first one, he receives the reply that, "I am laying bricks." Turning to a second bricklayer, he asks the same question and receives the reply that, "I am building a beautiful cathedral." Similarly, I believe focusing individuals on corporate success will inspire them to greater achievement and provide them with a more noble and meaningful work environment. And as I have suggested, it will be good for the organization as well. Interestingly, the great philosopher, Plato, recognized this thousands of years ago in his book, *Republic*.[3] While intending his comments for the wider society, they appear equally applicable to industrial organizations.

> Life in society requires the concession of some part of the individual's sovereignty to the common order; and ultimately the norm of conduct becomes the welfare of the group. Nature will have it so, and her judgment is always final; a group survives, in competition or conflict with another group, according to its unity and power, according to the ability of its

> members to cooperate for common ends. And what better cooperation could there be than that each should be doing that which he can do best? This is the goal of organization which every society must seek if it would have life.

In summary, my proposed model consists of a systems way of working, enabled by new strategic leadership, a supporting culture, and strategy processes that bring the people together interdependently to create a desired destination for the whole organization, and to move it successfully to that desired future state. I do not suggest that I have a "magical way" to structure organizations that will assure everyone's future success. There are many alternatives for achieving organizational success, and some choices will be better for certain organizations. I believe, however, that the solution that I outline will benefit many organizations. It draws upon major discoveries of our times, and brings together the power of people, working together collaboratively, to achieve a set of shared, strategic results. For the people, this identification with the greater good of the organization provides them greater meaning and nobility of purpose, while for the overall organization, greater performance becomes a reality.

Outline of the Book

I will start with an introduction of systems theory, and, where appropriate, its relationship to the organizational system. To accomplish this, I will summarize the work of five esteemed authors that have written about these topics. Next, in Chapter 2, building upon the work of these authors, I will discuss in depth the main theme of the book. Some of the questions I will address are:

- What is strategic leadership? How does systems thinking favorably impact strategic leadership?
- How does the leader manage and influence the organization as system?
- What is the role of culture in the organization as system?
- How does the new proposed model affect organizational performance? Is there any evidence of enhanced performance?

In Chapter 3, I will discuss the new organization that emerges from the influence of systems thinking – namely, the organization as system. What does it look like and how does it differ from the traditional organization? Why has it taken us so long to realize its benefits?

In Chapter 4, I will first take strategy and describe its role in the organizational system. *It is important to note from the outset that my emphasis in this book will be on the strategy processes, as opposed to the thinking of strategy.* Many esteemed authors write about the most recent strategic initiatives and debate their merits. Currently, this includes topics such as agility, the lean enterprise, new business models, innovation, collaboration, digitalization and discontinuity theory. On the other hand, the literature, and resulting knowledge of the processes of strategy, have tended to be either ignored or treated very superficially.

I will begin by describing the strategy processes and detail the ways that the strategy creation process and the strategy execution process contribute to the success of the organizational system. The reader will see that the output from the strategy creation process is a shared set of corporate, long-term results that employees can understand and identify with. *By focusing the attention of employees on the desired state of the "whole," the strategy creation process becomes a main enabler of the systemic nature of the organization.* I will also draw upon my unique, practical experience with a number of strategy tools. The tools bring people and groups together to enable clear strategic choices about the desired organizational results and the means to achieve them.

The strategy execution process in Chapter 5 will continue our discussion, and I will address the reasons for its monumental failures. I will then introduce a strategy execution process that both reinforces and uniquely builds upon the system characteristics of the organization.

After my discussion of strategy, in Chapter 6 I will turn to the role of organizational culture. In this section I will define culture and look at its unique interaction with the organizational system. Case study examples will emphasize the importance of culture on organizational performance. A major question for some will be, "How do I determine if my existing culture is an enabler, or an inhibitor to the success of the organizational system, and what do I do about it if it is not?" We will discuss this, and, additionally, will discuss case studies that bear on this question.

In Chapter 7, we will return to our discussion of leadership of the organization as system and look at how we can develop this capability. We have argued that this form of leadership is different from traditional forms, and while we will have focused on leadership at the top of the organization, we will turn to discuss the importance of leadership at all levels of the organization. How do we accomplish this? I will provide some unique ways that this can be accomplished.

Concluding, I will summarize our observations and describe specific steps leaders can take to put the lessons of this book into action. I will describe how to get started on relevant ideas, some of the obstacles that will stand in the way of implementation, and how to deal with these latter issues.

Intended Audience

This book is intended primarily for academics and consultants, and through their auspices, the students and clients that they serve. I am hopeful, of course, that the ideas expressed in the book will ultimately reach those most in need – namely, industrial organizations. Corporations of all sizes will benefit from this content. As I have briefly stated, this book looks at an interdependent way of working among individuals and groups, enabled by an organizational culture that supports that way of working, and strategy processes that focus the company on a shared set of organizational results. This same formula applies both to very large organizations and to small organizations. While implementation may be more complex for the larger organization, both have the same needs as I have described.

The formula that I describe in this book also applies to public, private and nonprofit corporations. Once again, these entities would benefit from having individuals working together interdependently for the good of their overall organization.

Lastly, the model that I describe in this book also applies to groups within corporations. Functional groups, for example, would benefit from individuals in the group working together interdependently for the overall good of the group. The overall good of the group could be stated as the mission of the group and/or its goals. As with the other entities I have just named, strategy processes and an empowering culture will enable successful achievement of the group's desired results.

Before closing this section, it might also be appropriate to discuss who other interested readers of this book might be. As I have stated, academics and consultants will be the primary targets, while senior business managers will best be able to put the ideas in this book into action. How will levels below the executive level profit from this book? Clearly, there is much to be learned for those who aspire one day to be a senior executive. I believe, however, that there are other ways that individuals lower in the organization can influence the overall corporation. Later, in the chapter on leadership, I will outline how this can be done and give examples of individuals and groups who have already accomplished this.

Finally, it is important to point out that this book has been designed to offer readers, based upon their needs and interests, options on the chapters that offer them the greatest value. A number of the chapters can stand alone and deliver great value. These are as follows:

Contributions of Leading Authors to General Systems Theory (Chapter 1)

Individuals interested in learning about systems theory will derive significant benefit from some of the greatest authors on the subject.

The Strategy Processes (Chapters 4 and 5)

From my extensive professional experience in the field of strategy, I have learned that there is a tremendous dearth of strategy knowledge at the senior levels of corporations. While there is no shortage of good, creative strategic ideas at the latter level, the knowledge to use the strategy processes to galvanize the whole organization is sadly missing. There is much practical knowledge to be gained about this problem and its solution from the chapters on strategy.

Organizational Culture (Chapter 6)

Like strategy, there is great confusion in business circles about culture. Readers will gain much practical knowledge about the subject from this chapter and from the very interesting case studies that are presented. And as I will discuss, there is often great confusion between legitimate strategy problems and underlying cultural problems that masquerade as strategy problems.

References

1. In this book, I will use the phrase "systems thinking" to refer to the general, wide body of knowledge associated with the study of systems. Classically, the phrase "General Systems Theory" (GST) has been used in the same way. While "systems thinking" appears to have more popular acceptance in contemporary circles, the reader will find me using both phrases interchangeably in this book.
2. Martin Seligman, *Flourish* (Simon & Schuster, 2011).
3. Quoted in: Will Durant, *The Story of Philosophy* (Washington Square Press, 1926).

1 A Summary of the Systems Theory Contributions of Leading Authors

I wish to give special mention to the following chapter. As I stressed in the section on "Intended Audience," this is one of the chapters that can stand alone and be of great benefit to those seeking to gain a basic understanding of General Systems Theory (GST). In my experience, the latter is probably a very large group.

In my sessions at Santa Clara University, I will often talk about systems, and in the process, stop and ask the participants, "By the way, what is a system?" It is not uncommon to be met with blank stares. Eventually, someone will offer an answer and others will join in the discussion, but it usually requires me to finally define and describe a system to them.

In this chapter, I will briefly summarize the major work of five authors – Ludwig von Bertalanffy, Fritjof Capra, Margaret Wheatley, Russell Ackoff and Gareth Morgan. Each of them in their own way has contributed to the foundation and development of systems theory and to my thinking. My purpose in this section is threefold: (1) to help the reader understand the basics of systems theory; (2) to especially highlight any discussions of the authors on the "organization as system;" and (3) to solidify my argument that a new form of organization is badly needed to address the current times. The reader will see powerful, convincing arguments that the existing machine model of organization is obsolete.

In the section that follows, I have often chosen to use the exact words of the authors, rather than paraphrase or interpret them. I believe this is necessary in order to preserve their original meaning and to provide the reader the opportunity to see firsthand the richness of their comments.

Lastly, the reader may ask why I am not using more current sources in this chapter. In my opinion, there has been nothing, more recently, to replace or enhance the quality of the material that I will present.

Ludwig von Bertalanffy

General Systems Theory was originally proposed in 1936 by Austrian biologist, Ludwig van Bertalanffy. In 1968, he wrote the book, *General Systems Theory*,[1] which has become the informal "Bible" of the discipline. In the book, he says the following:

> There are many instances where identical principles were discovered several times because the workers in one field were unaware that the theoretical structure required was already well-developed in some other field. General Systems Theory will go a long way towards avoiding such unnecessary duplication of labor.

Recognizing these benefits for the sciences is one of his main contributions.

Prior to Bertalanffy, the focus had been on individual components of a system and the belief that each component could be analyzed as an independent entity. The components could also be added linearly to describe the total system. Bertalanffy's view was that a system is characterized by the interactions of its components and those interactions are nonlinear.

Following are several concepts and quotes developed by Bertalanffy that will serve us as an introduction to General Systems Theory and that will have a subsequent impact later in our discussion of the "Leadership of the Organization as System."

First of all, we see Bertalanffy's belief that General Systems Theory will be far-reaching and will have a very broad impact on a gamut of disciplines. He also introduces the premise that GST is a significant new worldview.

> What may be obscured in these developments – important as they are – is the fact that systems theory is a broad view which far transcends technological problems and demands, a re-orientation that has become necessary in science in general and in the gamut of disciplines from physics and biology to the behavioral and social sciences and to philosophy. It is operative, with varying degrees of success and exactitude, in various realms, and heralds a new worldview of considerable impact.[2]

Later, he adds:

> Modern technology and society have become so complex that traditional ways and means are not sufficient anymore but approaches of a holistic or systems, and generalist or inter-disciplinary nature became necessary.... There can be no dispute that these are essentially "systems" problems, that is, problems of interrelations of a great number of variables.[3]

Bertalanffy continues with the theme of the need for General Systems Theory, its focus on "wholeness," and again, its benefits for both the physical and social sciences.

> Similar general conceptions and viewpoints have evolved in various disciplines of modern science. While in the past, science tried to explain observable phenomena by reducing them to an interplay of elementary units investigatable independently of each other, conceptions appear in contemporary science that are concerned with what is somewhat vaguely termed 'wholeness,' i.e., problems of organization, phenomena not resolvable into

> local events, dynamic interactions manifest in the difference of behavior of parts when isolated or in a higher configuration, etc.; In short, systems of various orders not understandable by investigation of the respective parts in isolation.[4]

Continuing:

> Conceptions and problems of this nature have appeared in all branches of science, irrespective of whether inanimate things, living organisms, or social phenomena are the object of study. This correspondence is the more striking because the developments in the individual sciences were mutually independent, largely unaware of each other, and based upon different facts and contradicting philosophies. They indicated general change in scientific attitude and conceptions.[5]

In my introduction, I mentioned that when summarizing the contributions of various authors to the field of General Systems Theory, I would highlight those quotes that deal particularly with the organization as system. Following is an example of such a quote.

> While sociology (and presumably history) deals with informal organizations, another recent development is the theory of formal organizations, that is, structures planfully instituted, such as those of an Army, bureaucracy, business enterprise, etc. This theory is 'framed in a philosophy which accepts the premise that the only meaningful way to study organization is to study it as a system,' systems analysis treating 'organization as a system of mutually dependent variables;' therefore 'modern organization theory leads almost inevitably into a discussion of general systems theory'.[6]

Following is a very interesting quote that talks about the role of hierarchy in the general theory of systems. Contemporary thinking has tended to see the hierarchy as an unwanted vestige of the past. One of the challenges that modern-day organizations face is dealing with the question of the relevance of the hierarchy for their organization.

> The above considerations pertain particularly to a concept or complex of concepts which indubitably is fundamental in the general theory of systems: that of *hierarchic order*. We presently see the universe as a tremendous hierarchy, from elementary particles to atomic nuclei, to atoms, molecules, high-molecular compounds, to the wealth of structures (electronic and light-microscopic) between molecules in cells, to cells, organisms and beyond to supra-individual organizations.[7]

As we investigate the organization as system, how do we reconcile the role of hierarchy? Is there a value-added role for it that we have not as yet identified? Later, I will discuss these questions.

Some of the concepts that Bertalanffy discusses in relationship to systems theory are: "open and closed systems," and "equifinality." He defines a closed system as one that is isolated from its environment. Contrasting this, he defines an "open system" as one that is open to its environment. He defines equifinality in the following manner:

> In any closed system, the final state is unequivocally determined by the initial conditions... If either the initial conditions or the processes are altered, the final state will also be changed. This is not so in open systems. Here, the same final state may be reached from different initial conditions and in different ways. This is what is called equifinality.[8]

We can see the influence of these concepts on the corporation. Clearly, the latter is an "open system," open to the environment that contains its customers, suppliers, markets and competition. We also see the concept of equifinality at work as, for example, objectives being achieved in a myriad of ways, using varying inputs. Creativity depends upon it.

Fritjof Capra

The book that has had the greatest influence on my interest in systems theory is *The Turning Point*.[9] Written in 1982 by Fritjof Capra, a physicist in Berkeley, California, it describes a cultural revolution affecting our worldview and a myriad of related disciplines. Early in the book, Fritjof mentions problems facing our society and the inability of intellectuals to deal with them.

> None of them, however, identified the real problem that underlies our crisis of ideas: the fact that most academics subscribe to narrow perceptions of reality which are inadequate for dealing with the major problems of our time. These problems, as we shall see in detail, are systemic problems, which mean that they are closely interconnected and interdependent. They cannot be understood within the fragmented methodology characteristic of our academic disciplines and government agencies. Such an approach will never resolve any of our difficulties but will merely shift them around in the complex web of social and ecological relations.[10]

The central theme of *The Turning Point* is perhaps best stated in the following quote:

> In contrast to the mechanistic Cartesian view of the world, the world view emerging from modern physics can be characterized by words like organic, holistic and ecological. It might also be called a systems view, in the sense of general systems theory. The universe is no longer seen as a machine, made up of a multitude of objects, but has to be pictured as one indivisible, dynamic whole whose parts are essentially interrelated and can be understood only as patterns of a cosmic process.[11]

Here we also see Capra's outline of his book. He will proceed to build a strong argument for the paradigm shift that we are seeing from the Newtonian/Cartesian world, which has dominated thinking for hundreds of years, to the contemporary view dominated by new physics thinking and systems theory. He will look in detail at these worldviews and examine how they have impacted the biomedical model, psychology, economics and human health.

Along the way, Capra discusses some concepts that will be useful for us later when we discuss the organization as system. One of those concepts is the holon, a concept developed by Arthur Koestler. Here is how Capra weaves this latter concept into his own thinking.

> Arthur Koestler has coined the word 'holon' for these subsystems which are both wholes and parts, and he has emphasized that each holon has two opposite tendencies: an integrative tendency to function as part of the larger whole, and a self-assertive tendency preserve its individual autonomy. In a biological or social system each holon must assert its individuality in order to maintain the system's stratified order, but it must also submit to the demands of the whole in order to make the system viable. These two tendencies are opposite but complementary. In a healthy system – an individual, a society or an ecosystem – there is a balance between integration and self-assertion. This balance is not static but consists of a dynamic interplay between the two complementary tendencies, which makes the whole system flexible and open to change.[12]

Capra's definition of the mechanistic view of the world that we are leaving is instructive for our later discussions.

> For two and a half centuries physicists have used the mechanistic view of the world to develop and refine the conceptual framework known as classical physics. They have based their ideas on the mathematical theory of Isaac Newton, the philosophy of René Descartes, and the scientific methodology advocated by Francis Bacon.... Matter was thought to be the basis of all existence, and the material world was seen as a multitude of separate objects assembled into a huge machine. Like human-made machines, the cosmic machine was thought to consist of elementary parts. Consequently it was believed that complex phenomena could always be understood by reducing them to their basic building blocks and by looking for the mechanisms through which these interacted. This attitude, known as reductionism, has become so deeply ingrained in our culture that it has often been identified with the scientific method.[13]

In a later section, Capra describes several aspects of systems theory. His emphasis on the "whole" and how it is different from the sum of the parts, differs greatly from our contemporary view of corporations and their emphasis on individual functions and departments.

> The activity of systems involves a process known as transaction – the simultaneous and mutually interdependent interaction between multiple components. Systemic properties are destroyed when a system is dissected, either physically or theoretically, into isolated elements. Although we can discern individual parts in any system, the nature of the whole is always different from the mere sum of its parts. Another important aspect of systems is their intrinsically dynamic nature. Their forms are not rigid structures but are flexible yet stable manifestations of underlying processes.[14]

Earlier, we cited Bertalanffy's view of the hierarchy. He stated that the hierarchy is present everywhere in nature and is not in conflict with systems theory. Capra defines the role of hierarchy somewhat differently. Later, I will attempt to reconcile these two diverse points of view and how they impact the modern-day organization.

> The multi-leveled structure of living organisms, like any other biological structure, is a visible manifestation of the underlying processes of self-organization. At each level there is a dynamic balance between self-assertive and integrative tendencies, and all holons act as interfaces and relay stations between systems levels. Systems theorists sometimes call this pattern of organization hierarchical, but that word may be rather misleading for the stratified order observed in nature. The word hierarchy referred originally to the government of the Church. Like all human hierarchies, this ruling body was organized into a number of ranks according to levels of power, each rank being subordinate to one at the level above it. In the past the stratified order of nature has often been misinterpreted to justify authoritarian social and political structures.
>
> To avoid confusion we may reserve the term hierarchy for those fairly rigid systems of domination and control in which orders are transmitted from the top down.... By contrast, most living systems exhibit multilevel patterns of organization characterized by many intricate and nonlinear pathways along which signals of information and transaction propagate between all levels, ascending as well as descending.[15]

Gareth Morgan

In the book, *Images of Organization*,[16] Gareth Morgan, a leading pioneer in organizational theory, provides us a fascinating look at organizations. Using metaphor as an organizing theme, he devotes a chapter each to descriptions of organizations as machines, as organisms, as brains, as cultures, as political systems, as psychic prisons, as flux and transformation, and as instruments of domination. While arguing for the validity of each viewpoint, his main point is that organizations contain elements of each of these models, and that it is important for executives, consultants, and others, to view organizations as made up of many diverse elements. For our purposes, we will see that

Gareth's discussion of the organization as organism is close to the theme of this book.

Gareth begins his book with a chapter on the organization as machine. We have already seen this theme in Fritjof Capra's work. Being fair to his models, Gareth provides both the benefits and disadvantages of each one. For example, he lists the following strengths of the machine metaphor.

- "Set goals and objectives and go for them."
- "Organize rationally, efficiently, and clearly."
- "Specify every detail so that everyone will be sure of the jobs that they have to perform."
- "Plan, organize, and control, control, control."[17]

He goes on to indict the functional organization in a number of ways. Contrary to the systems view that would have the functions viewing themselves as an enabling resource of the enterprise, Gareth sees the following occurring.

> The difficulty of achieving effective responses to changing circumstances is often further aggravated by the high degree of specialization in different functional areas within the organization (e.g., production, marketing, finance, product engineering). Interdepartmental communications and coordination are often poor, and people often have a myopic view of what is occurring, there being no overall grasp of the situation facing the enterprise as a whole. As a result the actions encouraged by one element of the organization often entail negative consequences for others, so that one element ends up working against the interests of another.[18]

Continuing with his criticism of the functional organization, Gareth hits upon one of the major reasons that new ways of working are needed in our times. He mentions that letting everyone know what is expected of them has its advantages, but has its problems "when the organization faces changing circumstances that call for initiative and flexibility in response."

He goes further to say the following.

> Mechanistic organization discourages initiative, encouraging people to obey orders and keep their place rather than to take an interest in, challenge, and question what they are doing. People in the bureaucracy who question the wisdom of conventional practice are viewed more often than not as troublemakers. Therefore, apathy often reigns, as people learn to feel powerless about problems which collectively they understand and ultimately have the power to solve.[19]

Finally, he summarizes his thoughts about the organization as machine.

> Mechanistic approaches to organization have proved incredibly popular, partly because of their efficiency in the performance of certain tasks, but

> also because of their ability to reinforce and sustain particular patterns of power and control. The machine metaphor has special appeal for individuals and groups who wish to exercise a close control over people and their activities.... However, there can be little doubt that the increasing rate of societal flux and change poses many problems for organizations based upon mechanical designs. Mechanistic organizations may well in the end prove to be but one specific kind of organization, generated by, yet only imperfectly suited to, the requirements of the mechanical age. Now that we are entering an age with a completely new technological base drawn on microelectronics, new organizational principles are likely to become of increasing importance.[20]

Reading Gareth Morgan's strong indictment of the machine model of organization, one has to wonder how it continues to survive in our modern age in so many companies. Later, we will discuss the reasons for this continued success.

In his following chapter, Gareth Morgan discusses the metaphor of the organization as organism. In this latter chapter, Gareth incorporates several ideas about General Systems Theory.

Throughout the chapter, Gareth gives credit to a number of organizational theories that emerged in the 20th century. He mentions, for example, the Hawthorne studies work that was conducted in the 1920s and 1930s. With the Hawthorne studies work, a new theory of organization began to emerge, built on the idea that individuals and groups, like biological organisms, operate most effectively only when their needs are satisfied. According to Gareth, during the 1960s and 1970s, further work on the design of work was done. This led to a focus on "social/technical systems," a term developed in the 1950s by members of the Tavistock Institute of Human Relations in England to capture the interdependent qualities of the social and technical aspects of work.

Later in the chapter, Gareth introduces the concept of General Systems Theory and gives credit to Bertalanffy for giving it its main inspiration. As with other authors that we have already mentioned, Gareth says the following: "The systems approach builds on the principle that organizations, like organisms, are open to their environment and must achieve an appropriate relation with an environment if they are to survive."

Next, Gareth introduces principles of General Systems Theory that have been derived from the study of biological systems, and now are used by some in the analysis of organizations as systems.[21] Later, we will take a more detailed look at which of these principles are most important in the study of the organization as system. *(I have included my personal comments with the following principles.)*

1. **Open System.** We have previously defined this concept. It is one in which the system is "open" to its environment. We see this concept in the work of multiple authors.
2. **Homeostasis.** This concept refers to self-regulation and the ability to maintain a steady state.

3. **Entropy/negative entropy.** Closed systems are entropic in that they have a tendency to deteriorate and run down. Open systems, on the other hand, attempt to sustain themselves by importing energy to try and offset these tendencies.
4. **Structure, function, differentiation and integration.** In a system, these are all interrelated.
5. **Requisite variety.** This principle states that the internal regulatory mechanisms of a system must be as diverse as the environment with which it is trying to deal. For only by incorporating required variety into internal controls can a system deal with the variety and challenge posed by its environment.
6. **Equifinality.** In an open system, there may be many different ways of arriving at a given end-state.
7. **System evolution.** For a system to evolve, it must depend on its ability to move to more complex forms of differentiation and integration, greater variety in the system facilitating its ability to deal with challenges and opportunities posed by the environment.

Returning again to some of the organizational theories that have influenced our current thinking, Gareth introduces the concept of "contingency theory." In summary, this concept says: "There is no one best way of organizing. The appropriate form depends on the kind of task or environment with which one is dealing." Two British researchers, Tom Burns and G.M. Stalker, are given credit for their contributions to this theory. In their work, they established a continuum between "mechanistic" and "organic" approaches to organization and management.

Gareth Morgan gives credit to Paul Lawrence and Jay Lorsch, Harvard researchers, who further developed contingency theory. They built their research around two principal ideas. "First that different kinds of organizations are required to deal with different market and technological conditions." Their second point was, "organizations that operate in uncertain and turbulent environments need to achieve a higher degree of internal differentiation, for example, between departments, than those environments that are less complex and more stable." In effect, the study by Lawrence and Lorsch showed that styles of organizations may need to have variance between organizational subunits because of the detailed characteristics of their subenvironments. They went on to add that an "appropriate degree of integration was also needed to tie the differentiated parts together again."

The contributions of Lawrence and Lorsch will be significant when we later discuss the role of departments in the systemic organization. We have already argued that contemporary departments continue to operate in a mechanistic fashion. Yet, we see from the work of Lawrence and Lorsch a possible model that would differentiate the departments according to environmental demands, while at the same time, integrating those departments in some manner. Perhaps, as we will discuss, there are strategic and cultural ways to provide this integration.

In a later section, Gareth makes the following statement:

> Between the 1960s and the 1980s hundreds of research studies have further addressed the job of specifying organizational characteristics and their success in dealing with different tasks and environmental conditions. The studies have added rich insight to the mechanistic – organic continuum developed by Burns and Stalker.

He mentions the work of Henry Mintzberg, for example, who identified five configurations of organization: the machine bureaucracy, the divisional form, the professional bureaucracy, the simple structure, and the adhocracy. To this list, we could add the Shamrock organization of Charles Handy and the matrix organization, which was popular at my own Digital Equipment Corporation. As we shall see later, however, most of these efforts dealt with the structure of the organization. Later, we will discuss the importance of other elements in affecting the ultimate well-being of the organization. The systemic organization depends vitally on interactions, depends on the interaction of organizational structure with items such as its culture, its people and its strategy. Actually, Gareth Morgan makes this very point when later he discusses a number of questions dealing with the relations between organization and environment and adds the following:

> In asking these questions we are building on the idea that the organization consists of interrelated subsystems of a strategic, human, technological, structural, and managerial nature, which need to be internally consistent and adapted to environmental conditions.[22]

Later, I will introduce a framework that incorporates these latter elements as part of an organization's operating model.

In the closing pages of the chapter on the organization as organism, Gareth prepares us for a future discussion that we must have about the organization as system. He says the following:

> While organizations may at times be highly unified, with people in different departments working in a selfless way for the organization as a whole, they may at other times be characterized by schism and major conflict. The organismic metaphor has had a subtle yet important impact on our general thinking by encouraging us to believe that the unity and harmony characteristic of organisms can be achieved in organizational life. We often tend to equate organizational well-being with a state of unity where everyone is pulling together.[23]

To this, he adds the following:

> As will become apparent from discussion in chapter 6, where we will be examining organizations as political systems, the emphasis upon unity

rather than conflict as the normal state of organization, may be an inherent weakness of the organismic metaphor.

Given such fragmentation, while there may be a general consensus about overall goals, there is often considerable disagreement about specific objectives, since at this level the interests of individuals and their subunits often become paramount. The organization as a whole is thus often obliged to function with a minimal kind of consensus. This allows the organization to survive while recognizing the diversity of the aims and aspirations of its members. The organization often has to be content with satisfactory rather than optimal solutions to problems, with negotiation and compromise becoming more important than technical rationality.[24]

The foregoing quotes introduce a touch of reality into the merits of my proposed model. Will I be able to address the concerns that Gareth Morgan presents, or will the conflict that he describes as the normal state of organizations prevail?

Before closing our discussion of Gareth Morgan's book, *Images of Organization*, it might be worthwhile to remember that his main point is that there are many different ways to view an organization. For him, no one metaphor is the ultimate answer. Strength lies in being able to see the organization as a complex tapestry of elements that present themselves at various times under varying conditions. We will address this argument later in our section on "Organization as System."

Margaret Wheatley

In her book, *Leadership and the New Science*,[25] Meg Wheatley, organizational consultant and Associate Professor at Brigham Young University, continues themes that we have heard from some of the authors whose thinking I have previously summarized. Like Fritjof Capra, for example, she assails the model of Newtonian Mechanics that has influenced our organizations for three to four centuries. For her, we need to look at the new sciences, such as quantum physics, chaos theory and evolutionary biology, and examine their impact on our contemporary organizations. While she does not specifically highlight General Systems Theory, we will see that she incorporates many of its elements into her discussion.

The theme of her book, and one that I use in this book, is that a new worldview has been derived from the natural sciences. Here are her words describing the departure from the Newtonian worldview.

But my focus on science is more than a personal interest. Each of us lives and works in organizations designed from Newtonian images of the universe. We manage by separating things into parts, we believe that influence occurs as a direct result of force exerted from one person to another, we engage in complex planning for a world that we keep expecting to be predictable, and we search continually for better methods of objectively perceiving the world. These assumptions as I explain in Chapter 2, come

> to us from 17th-century physics, from Newtonian Mechanics. They are the base from which we design and manage organizations, and from which we do research in all the social sciences. Intentionally or not, we work from a worldview that has been derived from the natural sciences.[26]

She further expands Newtonian Mechanics and contrasts it with the new science in the following manner.

> In the machine model, one must understand parts. Things can be taken apart, dissected literally or representationally (as we have done with business functions and academic disciplines), and then put back together without any significant loss. The assumption is that by comprehending the workings of each piece, the whole can be understood. The Newtonian model of the world is characterized by materialism and reductionism—a focus on things rather than relationships, and a search, in physics, for the basic building blocks of matter. In new science, the underlying currents are a movement toward holism, toward understanding the system as a system and giving primary value to the relationships that exist among seemingly discrete parts.[27]

As with some of the other authors that we have discussed, Margaret specifically refers to the organization as system in the following paragraph:

> We are beginning to recognize organizations as systems, construing them as 'learning organizations' and crediting them with some type of self-renewing capacity….My own experience suggests that we can forego the despair created by such common organizational events as change, chaos, information overload, and cyclical behaviors if we recognize that organizations are conscious entities, possessing many of the properties of living systems.[28]

A major theme that I will stress in this book is that in viewing the organization as a system, there is great resulting advantage in being able to move that system as a whole. Margaret makes a similar point.

> We have broken things into parts and fragments for so long, and have believed that was the best way to understand them, that we are unequipped to see a different order that is there, moving the whole….. The challenge for us is to see beyond the innumerable fragments to the whole. Stepping back far enough to appreciate how things move and change as a coherent entity.[29]

Margaret continues her theme of drawing implications of the new science on the way that contemporary organizations can work. In the following passage, she uses a jazz metaphor to describe how leaders might work.

> Those who have used music metaphors in describing leadership, particularly jazz metaphors, are on a quantum track. Improvisation is the saving skill. As leaders, we play a crucial role in selecting the melody, setting the tempo, establishing the key, and inviting the players. But that is all we can do. The music comes from something we cannot direct, from a unified whole created among the players – a relational holism that transcends separateness. In the end, when it works, we sit back, amazed and grateful.[30]

Building further on the theme of relationships, she says the following. Later we will see the power of the strategy process in making this a reality.

> But there is an urgent challenge to create organizations that respond to this new world of relationships in which we act as grand evocateurs of reality. Our old views constrain us. They deprive us from engaging fully with this universe of potentialities.... Why would we avoid participation and worry only about its risks, when we need more and more eyes to evoke reality? Why would we resist the rich visions and strong futures that emerge when we come together to create the world?[31]

Earlier, Fritjof Capra introduced the concept of self-organization as a characteristic of a system. Margaret Wheatley builds on this concept and describes how human organizations can survive in turbulent environments. She refers to the role that culture plays in this and describes how it can provide the organization a source of independence from the chaotic changes that occur in the environment.

> These companies highlight a principle that is fundamental to all self-organizing systems, that of *self-reference*. In response to environmental disturbances that signal the need for change, the system changes in a way that remains consistent with itself in that environment.... In human organizations, a clear sense of identity – the values, traditions, aspirations, competencies, and culture that guide the operation – is the real source of independence from the environment. When the environment demands a new response, there is a reference point for change.[32]

In effect, we see a quality that we will build on later when we discuss the organization as system. We see that the system has a mechanism to ensure its stability, while at the same time permitting individuals within that system to creatively deviate. Self- reference provides individuals a strong reference point amidst changes that are permitted at local levels.

Earlier, we talked about the advantage of being able to move the whole system instead of its component parts. We will talk more about this later when we talk about strategy as an effective way to accomplish this. Margaret underscores this point as she describes the complexity of managing individual pieces of the organizational operation.

> But there is a way out of this fear of complexity and we find it as we step back and refocus our attention on the whole. When we give up myopic attention to details and stand far enough to observe the movement of the total system, we develop a new appreciation for what is required to manage a complex system.[33]

With such an emphasis these days on innovation and its basis for competitive advantage, we see Margaret continue with emphasis on the innovation that results from the relationships and connections within the organizational system.

> Innovation is fostered by information gathered from new connections; from insights gained by journeys into other disciplines or places; from active, collegial networks and fluid, open boundaries. Innovation arises from ongoing circles of exchange, where information is not just accumulated or stored, but created. Knowledge is generated anew from connections that weren't there before. When this information self-organizes, innovations occur, the progeny of information-rich ambiguous environments.[34]

Margaret mentions another advantage of looking at organizations as whole systems – its use in solving problems. She says the following: "Is there an attempt to step back from the problem, to gain enough perspective so that its shape emerges under the myriad variables that influence it? Are people encouraged to look for themes and patterns, rather than isolated causes?"

Before moving on to our last author, it might be worthwhile to summarize a few key points from Margaret's book. Margaret Wheatley applies concepts and principles from new science to ways that contemporary organizations might behave and benefit from those behaviors. Many of her thoughts assume the organization as system. New science gives us the principles; General Systems Theory organizes these principles into a way of thinking that applies to many different sciences and to many disciplines.

Russell Ackoff

Russell Ackoff, the esteemed former Dean Emeritus of the Wharton School, will be our last author whose thoughts I will summarize. Of all the authors, he will have the most to say about the organization as a system. Like the previous authors, he also discusses the machine model and is critical of its application in contemporary times.

Russell begins his book, *The Democratic Corporation*,[35] by discussing three historical stages that have characterized the enterprise. As mentioned, he discusses the enterprise as a machine. In his second stage, he discusses the enterprise as an organism. During this stage, the enterprise had survival as its purpose and growth was essential for its continued survival. "Biological metaphors, such as the chief executive being called the head of the organization, and concepts, such as, viable, healthy, sick, paralyzed and energetic, also came to be applied." In Ackoff's third stage, he identified the enterprise as a social system. This is the stage most closely related to my concept of the organization as system.

Leading into the nature of systems, Ackoff says the following. You could argue that the following quote comes very close to the broad theme of my book.

> Social systemic thinking requires fundamental changes in the way work is designed and organized and in the way the resulting organizations are managed. To know what changes are required and to understand why they are required, in turn requires an understanding of the nature of *systems* generally and the nature of the *social* systems in particular.[36]

After World War II, he goes on to say, the concept of system became a focal point not only in organizational and managerial thinking but also in science, philosophy and public affairs.

In a brilliant section on part-part interactions, Ackoff begins to lay the foundation for the way that the systemic organization differs from more traditional organizations. In our later discussion of the organization as system, we will build on his thinking.

Following are several notable quotes that highlight the challenges that industrial organizations face in getting the parts of their organization to work together in support of the whole.

> The performance of a system obviously depends on the performance of its parts, but an important, if not the most important, aspect of a part's performance is how it interacts with other parts to affect the performance of the whole. How part of a system performs when considered independently of the system of which it is a part is irrelevant to its performance in the system of which it is a part. A part that works well when considered separately may not work well when interacting with other parts of a system; the parts may not fit together well. A Rolls–Royce engine may not fit into a Volkswagen.... For these reasons, effective corporate management must focus on the interactions of its parts rather than on their actions taken separately. However, current organizational design and modes of management focus on the actions of corporate parts rather than their interactions. It is assumed that if each part works well when considered separately, the corporation as a whole will, but this is not true.[37]

In a very bold statement, which challenges our ideas about leadership, he adds:

> Supervision and command are the management of actions; coordination and integration are the management of interactions, and this requires leadership. The exercise of leadership does not necessarily require authority.[38]

In a later section, Ackoff describes the need for generalists who understand the interplay of skills, technologies and functions. This thinking is a departure from the specialization prevalent in most corporations and universities. He also takes aim at several things that are key to our concept of the organization as system – namely, how departments plan and how value is established between the parts and whole of the organization.

> Nevertheless, the way most enterprises are organized and managed, and the way managers are educated, fly in the face of this property of systems. For example, in most corporate planning each organizational unit initially plans for itself independently of any others. These plans are subsequently adjusted to each other and aggregated. However, the adjustments are usually directed at removing conflict between or among the parts, not at maximizing their cooperation and collective performance.
>
> Synergy is an increase in the value of the parts of a system that derives from their being parts of the system – that is, from their interactions with other parts of the system. Such an increase in value can occur only if the parts can do something together that they cannot do alone. Put another way, synergy requires an increase in the variety of behavior available to the parts of a system. Mechanistic and organismic concepts of an enterprise are variety-reducing; a social systemic concept alone is necessarily variety-increasing.[39]

Having discussed part-part interaction, Ackoff turns his attention to whole-part interactions. He also expresses the value between the enterprise and other outside systems that it interfaces with. *We see very prominently displayed here again the role of the strategic leader in the organization as system.*

> The value of a system and its parts may be increased through interactions of the whole and its parts, between or among the parts, and between or among the whole of the systems with which it forms larger systems. All three types of interaction must be managed effectively if an organization is to perform well.[40]

As we have seen, most of our authors consider the organization as machine model obsolete. Russell Ackoff states very clearly the reasons for this.

> Autocratic (mechanistically conceptualized) enterprises can be efficient in circumstances where the conditions to which they must react are limited in number, relatively simple, and predictable. However, such organizations are not able to cope effectively with unexpected and complex changes imposed on them. They cannot adapt rapidly and effectively, if at all, to such a turbulent environment as now prevails, one characterized, it will be recalled, by an increasing rate of change and complexity.[41]

Later, he summarizes and strengthens this argument.

> Enterprises conceptualized and managed as social systems, and their parts, can respond to the unpredictable changes inherent in turbulent environments and can deal effectively with increasing complexity. They can expand the variety of their behavior to match or exceed the variety of the behavior of their environments because of the freedom of choice that pervades them. They are capable not only of rapid and effective passive adaptation to change but also of active adaptation. They can innovate by perceiving and exploiting opportunities for change that are internally, not externally, stimulated.[42]

Ackoff summarizes his chapter on the "Emerging Concept of Enterprise" with several quotes that highlight the significant differences of the organization as a social system.

> Most managers are still unaware of the implications of the systemic properties of enterprises. Perhaps most important among these implications is the fact that the performance of a system is not the sum of the performances of its parts taken separately; it is the product of their interactions.... Enterprises are not currently organized to facilitate managers focusing on interactions, only on the actions of parts taken separately. Furthermore their compensation normally provides incentives only for improving the actions of parts, not their interactions.
>
> Improving the performance of the parts of a system taken separately may not, and often does not, improve the performance of the system taken as a whole. This implies that in designing a system the properties of the parts should be derived from the properties designed into the whole. Too frequently, the properties designed into an enterprise as a whole are derived from the properties of their parts.[43]

This concludes our chapter on the contributions of selected authors to GST. Before we proceed to the next chapter, however, we might conclude from what has been said that the machine model of organization is obsolete. Among other things, it no longer satisfies the needs of our rapidly changing, dynamic environment. The authors go on to argue that a systems way of working and structuring is a solution to the latter problem. For a summary of the characteristics of the machine model versus the systems model, see Table 1.1.

In Chapter 3, we will look at a proposed systems way of working in our discussion of the organization as system. *Later chapters will address what in my opinion is a major shortcoming of our authors' material – namely, while elegantly espousing General Systems Theory as a remedy for the machine model of organization and as a solution for the needs of our modern times, no one has presented a practical way to get to this organizational state.*

Table 1.1 A Summary of Machine Model Versus Systems Model

Features	*Machine Model*	*Systems Model*
Source	1700s, Newton and Descartes	1900s, quantum physics, GST
Philosophy	Reductionism, materialism	Holism
Structure	Functional	Systemic, functional with subsystems
Salient Features	Specialization, atomistic	Interdependence, collaborative
Strengths	Efficiency, control	Adaptability, innovation, learning
Weaknesses	Siloed, insular, lack of corporate perspective	Difficulty of implementation, political barriers
Contemporary Fit	Not suited for complexity, rate of change	Well-suited, needs proof of model
Part/Part Interaction	Transactional, variety-reducing	Synergy, variety-increasing
Part/Whole Interaction	Self-assertion of part	Holon: self-assertion of part, integration into whole

References

1. Ludwig von Bertalanffy, *General System Theory* (George Braziller, 1968).
2–8. Ibid.
9. Fritjof Capra, *The Turning Point* (Bantam Books, 1982).
10–15. Ibid.
16. Gareth Morgan, *Images of Organization* (Sage Publications, 1986).
17–24. Ibid.
25. Margaret J. Wheatley, *Leadership and the New Science* (Berrett-Koehler, 1992).
26–34. Ibid.
35. Russell L. Ackoff, *The Democratic Corporation* (Oxford University Press, 1994).
36–43. Ibid.

2 The New Strategic Leader

Introduction

I would like to start this chapter with a short story that perhaps will provide greater clarity about both the central figure in this book, i.e., the strategic leader, and the main theme of the book. It is the story of the origin of the symphony orchestra – part historical fact and part imagined.

The historical fact is that by the year 1607, we had in place the essence of today's symphony orchestra, composed of different instrument sections and lots of variety. The occasion was Claudio Monteverdi's performance of the opera, *Orfeo*, in which he had expressed, for the first time, the exact composition of instruments that should play in the opera. It is not hard to imagine, however, that this occurrence did not happen suddenly. Preceding it was probably a long period of experimentation with the model of solo instrumentation that had been in place for thousands of years. Further, we can assume that during this period of experimentation and evolution, certain leaders would occasionally surface with the vision of an orchestra that included various instruments playing the same piece of music together. These leaders most likely made the argument that the music that would be produced in this fashion would extend the capability of the individual instruments and enrich the resulting melodies.

Probably it wasn't easy at first. A style of working had to evolve – what today we would call a culture, and they had to have a process that got them to work together to create the shared end-state that, by now, they all envisioned. And we can probably guess that each musician found significant meaning by having a "part to play" in the scene that was unfolding.

Eventually, the symphony orchestra came together, guided by the past vision of a few great leaders and the contributions of many individual musicians. The resulting product of their joint efforts was to inspire generations that followed. In the following century, luminaries such as Mozart and Beethoven were to build upon these early efforts.

The foregoing story is a good example of the new strategic leader that I will be discussing in this chapter. This leader envisions a new kind of future and is able to successfully engage a diverse group of individuals and inspire them to work together to create this desired future state.

In Chapter 1, we looked at the General Systems Theory contributions of five esteemed authors. Where appropriate, I highlighted their views on the organization as system. What can we conclude from their writings? And what can we say about the organization as system that they, or others, have not already said? And lastly, what can we say about the impact of their thinking on the role of the strategic leader?

In the chapters that follow, we will see the merits of the model that I am proposing to enhance corporate performance. We will see systems thinking combine with strategy processes in new ways that bring out the best of each and accomplish the following:

- Create identity of the parts with the whole, i.e., of the functions with the enterprise.
- Create a shared set of corporate results that serve as the destination of the whole system.
- Enable major, performance-enhancing decisions. We will see new strategic insights emerge from the pattern-recognizing capability of systems thinking.
- Improve the execution success of strategic initiatives. I will introduce a unique execution model that brings individuals and groups together with their understanding of the strategy, their personal commitment to it, and finally, their performance against the metrics that have been established.

In this chapter, we will look at strategic leadership and investigate the influence that systems thinking (classically referred to as General Systems Theory) has on it. In order to properly position strategic leadership, we will first look at its origin. We will also look at related research that shows the potential of various types of leaders to adopt systems thinking. Next, I will introduce a model that highlights the central theme of the book. In the model, the "new strategic leader" is graphically shown with the elements that determine this enhanced role. And lastly, I will describe detailed actions that the strategic leader should put in place in order to successfully implement the model and to maximally derive the benefits that it provides.

Foundations of Strategic Leadership

We can define strategic leadership as the ability of an individual, or group, to lead the organization successfully to a desired future state. Using this definition, I wish to separate "strategic leadership" from the broad and general description of "leadership" that is found in the many books written on the subject. As I will describe, the strategic leader, inspired by systems thinking and using strategy processes, enables and manages a new form of working and thinking in the organization. He envisions the organization as a "whole," which through his influence, can be moved to a future, desirable place.

Our origins of strategic leadership go back to the military, where for thousands of years, success in warfare depended vitally on this capability. For example, in the *Art of War*, Sun Tzu said the following:

> All men can see the tactics whereby I conquer, but what none can see is the strategy out of which great victory is evolved.[1]

We can also use Sun Tzu's quote to introduce a distinction between our classical definition of strategy and my use of it in this book. In the foregoing quote, Sun Tzu may equate "strategy" with the thinking contained in his long-range plan. Generally, this use continues today in the vast number of books and articles on strategy. Instead, as I will outline, my emphasis will be on the processes that are used to create and execute the content. This latter usage in no way devalues the importance of the strategy content; rather, it uses "strategy" in a new and different way to address what I consider to be some of the major business challenges of our times.

We tend to associate strategic leadership with high-level positions. In the military, for example, we tend to see generals as the strategic leaders. In fact, the word "strategy" comes from the Greek word "strategos," which translates to, "the art of the general." Years of training, education and practical experience prepare generals for the strategic leadership role.

Whether through training/experience, or by virtue of an innate quality, strategic leaders tend to have the ability to see the pattern and the "big picture." Unlike others not similarly gifted, they tend not to get lost in detail. It is also noteworthy that, unlike business leaders, military strategic leaders both see the "big picture" and see the interdependent nature of the parts of the organization. For example, it is not unusual to see field Army forces supported by Air Force pilots, or Navy ships hosting Marine assault troops – in both cases, working together interdependently to accomplish the mission.

What can we say about business strategic leaders? In one of my programs at Santa Clara University, we used a questionnaire, the InQ,[2] to assess the thinking styles of seminar attendees. The questionnaire assessed five different styles: synthesist, idealist, analyst, pragmatist and realist. The idealist style corresponded closest to the "big picture" capabilities of the strategic leader that I have described. Over the years, we assessed over 700 students and found the idealist style dominant among senior leaders, while the analyst style tended to dominate among more junior audiences.[3] Later, in my chapter on developing the strategic leader, I will come back to the InQ as an instrument that can potentially be used for this developmental task.

If indeed, as my research suggests, senior business leaders are able to see the "big picture," why has that thinking not previously led to the organization being developed as an overall system? Did they not see the benefits? Were the inhibitors too great? Did they lack the means to accomplish this? In the next chapter, I will address these questions.

In summary, the new strategic leader, influenced by systems thinking, will see the organization as a whole. I believe that, like military leaders, she will also see the parts of the organization as interdependent elements of this whole. Further, she will envision that if she could influence an organization to operate in the latter mode, organizational performance would be greatly enhanced. I have suggested that the systemic strategic leader can indeed exert this influence through strategic and cultural means. In later chapters, we will look in detail at how this can be accomplished, but for now, let us take a closer look at the overall model that I am proposing.

A New Strategic Leadership Model

Systems occur naturally in nature, but need to be enabled in organizations. In Chapters 4 and 5, we will look at the main enablers of a systems way of working – namely the strategy processes. The model that I am proposing in this book, shown in Figure 2.1, also shows culture and leadership as enablers.

Figure 2.1 graphically illustrates the main theme of this book. In the figure, we see a systems way of working and thinking enabled by the strategy creation process and the strategy execution process. We see also that this new systems way of working and thinking is identified with the "whole," rather than with the parts of the organization.

In the center of the model, we see leadership and culture serving as enablers to this new pattern of work and thought. The central positioning also suggests that certain cultural and leadership elements need to be in place for the strategy processes to be effective. Let us briefly look here at the roles of leadership and culture in the model. Later, I will expand upon these two subject areas in a chapter devoted to each.

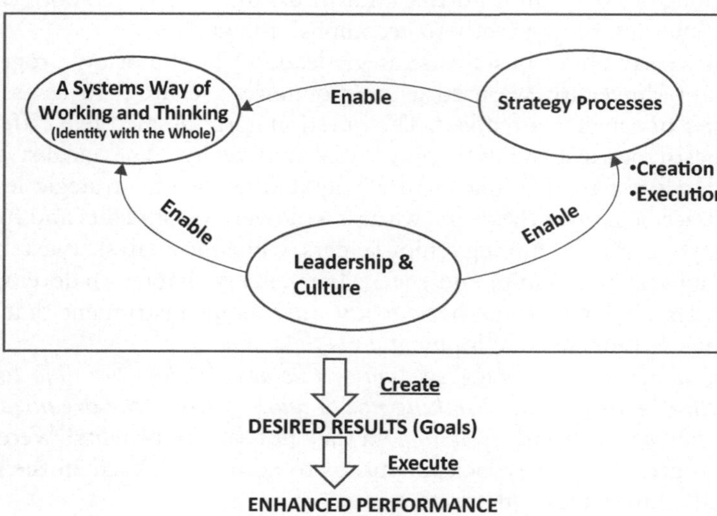

Figure 2.1 Strategic Leadership and Systems Thinking.

There are certain cultures that enable the interdependent, systems way of working that I have described. Generally, these cultures are participative, empowered and person-centered. Creativity tends to arise in this type of culture, as people feel trusted and see limitless opportunities for them to contribute to their organization's success. In the model shown in Figure 2.1, people from this type of culture value working with others in the strategy processes and feel unlimited in their potential to not just create a strategic plan, but rather, to create an exciting new future for the corporation.

I have argued that this book is different from the many books written about strategy. It is also different from the host of books written about generic leadership skills. This book is about a new form of leadership – one that manages the interactions between people and between groups. Like the orchestra leader in my opening story, he brings together the previously disconnected instruments, "into a vibrant tapestry of beautiful music."

Following are the particulars of this new form of strategic leadership. Later, in a separate chapter on leadership, I will expand upon this list and highlight it with case examples.

In order to enable and lead the organization as system, strategic leaders should do the following:

1. Leaders of the organizational system should get its members to focus on the "whole." This "whole" is the overall good of the enterprise. As I will further define, the latter is best represented by the long-term goals that members of the organization have helped create and which define success for the organization. We know from change theory that what leaders pay attention to is an effective way to get members of the organization to do the same; therefore, leaders should call constant attention to the "whole."
2. Strategic leaders should manage the interaction between the parts of the system. This is vastly different from managing, or overseeing, the parts themselves. Rather than focusing on the "goodness" of each part, the strategic leader sees enhanced organizational performance as the product of the interactions between parts of the organization and their contribution to the overall good of the corporation.
3. Leaders of the organizational system must become knowledgeable about strategy processes. In addition, they should take steps to embed this knowledge appropriately into their organization.
4. Leaders must also become knowledgeable about organizational culture. I have positioned a certain type of culture as an enabler to the organization as system. How do I, as leader, shape, build and embrace this kind of culture?
5. The strategy processes, as we have discussed, are powerful enablers for creating shared, desired organizational results, for creating identification of the members of the organization with these desired results, and for enabling the interdependent way of working to achieve them. Leaders must understand how to accomplish these steps.

6. I will argue in a later chapter that strategy is all about choices. Leaders of the organizational system must sometimes make difficult choices. In addition, they must clarify the choices that have been made. These actions will assist the formation of the collective efforts of the individual workers.
7. In addition to the steps that I have outlined, the organization as system also uses systems thinking to make better decisions and to more effectively solve problems. Leaders should both model this skill and develop it in the senior members of their organization.

With Figure 2.1, I have presented a graphic depiction of the main theme of the book. In discussing the model, I have also briefly discussed culture and leadership as enablers for a systems way of working. In Chapters 4 and 5, I will detail the strategy processes as enablers, and in Chapter 6, I will provide greater detail on organizational culture. At this point, one of my most successful case study examples might tie together for the reader how it is that leadership, culture and strategy processes enable a systems way of working, and indeed, enhance greater corporate performance. The seminal idea for the model that I propose in this book came originally from the work that I did with the subject client.

A Case Study Example of Enhanced Organizational Performance

One way that leaders can make the "whole" visible to the members of the organization is by showing them the interrelationships that exist, which, if understood, can make the company stronger and more successful. For me, the best example of this has been the founder of a company in the western United States. I came to know him in my consulting work and found him to be one of the most inspirational people I have ever met. I have told people that listening to him in speeches to his people was like a religious experience.

This person, whom in the interest of privacy, I will refer to as Mr. Entrepreneur, was an amazing visionary. He somehow saw his businesses as all interrelated. He started the company in the late 1920s and his first business was the potato business. At the time, potatoes were sorted manually in order to eliminate the poor ones from the good ones. The good ones were subsequently packaged and shipped to market. Mr. Entrepreneur found a way to use electric motors to do the sorting and contracted with individual farmers to perform this service for them.

Approximately ten years later, he developed a process to dehydrate onions and when World War II broke out in the 1940s, he signed a major contract with the military to dehydrate potatoes and to ship them to foreign theaters. This increased the demand for potatoes and led Mr. Entrepreneur to investigate ways that he could increase their yield. In turn, this led him to the fertilizer business, which became another major business for the company. The development of new businesses was not to stop here, however; Mr. Entrepreneur saw potato peels as possible livestock feed. This subsequently led him into the livestock business. Eventually, the company used potatoes to start producing

French fries, which, in turn, became a major business serving McDonalds and others.

Mr. Entrepreneur built a multibillion-dollar enterprise and ranks as one of the most successful entrepreneurs of all time. He challenged his people to follow his lead and also be very creative. I sat in sessions in which he would articulate his beliefs about entrepreneurship. Often, he would use an example of a project that had failed, but state how proud he was of the individual who, in the process, had just gotten some very valuable learning.

My initial work with the company was to do an information technology (IT) planning session with one of their divisions. This was a two-day event and had been initiated by the head of computing at the company. Present were all the senior officers of the division.

The division produced industrial chemicals and fertilizers. Fertilizer was one of their main products. My process started with discussions of the division's business strategy. Foremost in this discussion were the business goals that they wanted to achieve over the next five years. After achieving clarity on the desired business results that they wanted, the discussion turned to looking at ways that IT could help them achieve these results.

I remember vividly our discussion at the time about potential ways that information technologies might benefit their business. One of the executives in the planning session was the Vice President (VP) of Mining. His job dealt with extracting potassium phosphate from the ground and converting it into fertilizer. He commented that this was a very costly operation and often resulted in failure. He added that he didn't think information technology could help him with this.

Turning to the group, I asked if anyone had any ideas about how information technology could help the VP of Mining reduce costs in the work that he had just described. Subsequent discussions centered on the reasons for the high cost and they revealed that it was often difficult to find the exact location of the potassium phosphate deposit. Oftentimes, for example, a subterranean fault might undermine the exact location that had been previously predicted.

In any event, I was fascinated with the power of the group to arrive at a number of possible information technology solutions that could help the Vice President of Mining reduce his extraction costs. One of the solutions, for example, involved using artificial intelligence to do more accurate predictions of the locations of the ore deposits. This was not at the time a systemic organization arriving at creative solutions, but it does illustrate a quality that we have argued would result in a systemic organization. We would see people from different functions, creatively and interdependently interacting to find solutions that would impact the goals of the organization and, therefore, benefit the whole company. *As happened with my client company, this could perhaps happen in other settings, but it is in the formal, structured, strategy process that questions of such serious concern to the future of the organization emerge and can creatively be dealt with. The strategy process also places the latter discussions, as we have seen, within the context of the goals of the organization. In so doing, the decisions that result will have maximum potential to enhance the performance of the organization.*

In this case example, I have introduced the way that business strategy can enable a systems way of working. Let us continue now and see how leadership and organizational culture also played parts in this example.

The two-day planning session was highly successful. In fact, the head of computing, who had provided the initial leadership, was promoted to Chief Information Officer (CIO). In addition, his IT budget doubled in the ensuing years.

Subsequently, I was approached by the Corporate Director of Strategic Planning and asked if I would assist him with the corporate strategic plan. Of special concern to them at the time were a number of critical issues that potentially stood in the way of their future success.

Following the lead of the corporate Director of Strategic Planning, we focused on critical issues that stood in the way of the company's achievement of their strategic goals. After approximately four months of developing these critical issues, we were asked to present them to the Executive Committee. In total, there were approximately 23 of these barriers to success. The challenge was how to present these in a way that was intelligible and that could be acted upon by the Executive Committee. After some reflection and analysis on our part, we finally came up with the exhibit shown in Table 2.1. It occurred to us that most of the issues could be distilled into one root issue – namely, "What kind of a company do you want to be?" The following exhibit was to become the cornerstone of our presentation to the Executive Committee.

In the presentation, which was attended by the CEO, Division Presidents, and staff, we explained that many of the critical issues that they were experiencing came down to a choice between two different ways of thinking and acting. On the one hand was the original entrepreneurial culture of the company, with its emphasis on internal control, creativity, empowerment and

Table 2.1 What Kind of a Company Do You Want to Be?

Entrepreneurialism	*Professional Management*
Internal Controls	External Controls
Creativity	Conformity
Individual Autonomy	Central Control
Intuitive	Rational/Logical
Right Brain	Left Brain
"That Ol' Gut Feel"	Scientific Management
Decentralization	Centralization
Distributed Computing	Centralized Computing
Networks	Hierarchies
Adult-Adult	Parent-Child
Person-Centered	Organization-Centered
Product Differentiation	Low Cost Producer

individual autonomy. On the other hand was a professional management culture that stressed, among other things, external control, hierarchy, scientific management and top-down decision-making. Now that the company had grown to be a multibillion-dollar establishment, there were factions that felt stricter controls were necessary. Representative of this viewpoint was the Chief Financial Officer (CFO), who was heard to articulate the message that, "We want to be an entrepreneurial company, but with controls."

Using the exhibit, we explained that critical issues were masquerading as visible surface elements of this cultural clash. For example, the question of structure (should we be centralized or decentralized?), the question of strategy (should we compete on the basis of cost leadership or differentiation?) and questions of control (how much autonomy should the divisions have?) were all manifestations of the unresolved cultural conflict that was occurring.

As we continued our discussion with the Executive Committee, I explained that while some felt that it would be highly desirable, for example, to take the original entrepreneurial culture and to add aspects of the professional management culture to it, this isn't how culture worked. As I was to state,

> Gentlemen, this isn't Burger King. When it comes to culture, 'you can't have it your way.' If you impose tight controls on your existing culture, you will soon compromise the existing empowerment, initiative, risk-taking and creativity. Culture is like a tightly-woven fabric, and if you break it apart in the way that you suggest, you will destroy it.

To the credit of the executive team, they decided to stay with the existing entrepreneurial culture. They realized that their historical success had been based upon this culture and that there was no serious reason to change it.

We have now seen the roles that both culture and the strategy process played in bringing together multiple divisions to create a desired future direction for the company. What remains to be seen is the strong role that leadership played.

As I have stated, movement of the organizational "whole" to a desired future state is a critical element of organizational success. Leaders need to understand and put in place an effective strategy execution process that successfully moves the members of the organization to this desired destination. Engaging members of the organization in the strategy creation process is not enough; leaders must also "get them to the finish line."

The company in the western states turned out to be one of the best examples of strategic execution that I have ever seen. During the years when the Founding Chairman had become less active, a new CEO had been chosen. As I mentioned, I was involved with him and his direct reports in a strategic planning process. This process ended with a presentation to the CEO and his staff. I still remember clearly that when we talked about the execution of the plan, the CEO had stated very directly to his team that they would be reviewing the progress of the strategic plan at each of his staff meetings.

Some months later, I received a call from the CIO of the company, who related to me that the CEO wanted me to fly up and have breakfast with him. Not knowing what the purpose of the meeting was, I boarded a plane and went up to see him.

At the breakfast, the CEO started by thanking me for the help I had given them on their strategic plan. Inquiring, I asked him what had happened. He proceeded to tell me that they had just completed the best quarter in the company's history. Inquiring further, he told me that they had put in place everything that I had helped them put into the plan. Somewhat embarrassed by the praise, I responded, "Why are you thanking me; you are the ones that deserve all the credit?" It turns out they had indeed reviewed the progress of the plan at every staff meeting. *They went on subsequently to have the best year in this company's 60-year history.*

Summarizing the lessons from this case, we see in the foregoing example all the elements of the model that I am proposing in this book. First of all, we see the leadership of the legendary founder. He role-modeled a style of thinking and working that was years ahead of its time. Through his influence, a culture evolved that trusted people, was risk-taking, innovative and entrepreneurial. The strategy processes brought the people together interdependently to debate and make choices about the future they wanted for the company. Lastly, the leadership of the new CEO brought the people to the desired destination they had all worked together to create.

In the chapters that follow, I will describe the two elements that, along with leadership, are the two major components of the model I have proposed in this book. These are strategy and culture. First I will describe the role of strategy and describe its positive, enabling force – a focus that continues to be poorly missing in many organizations. The strategic influence comes from setting a direction for the organization that involves the people and makes it clear to everyone where the organization is going and their role in helping the organization get there. The cultural influence involves an organizational culture in which the people feel trusted and empowered, and as a result, unleash their creative energies in pursuit of the goals of the enterprise.

In effect, my model takes the characteristics of "whole systems change" and details how influencing a whole system depends vitally on getting people focused collaboratively on the shared results they seek, the means to achieve them, and the organizational fabric that makes this all possible.

In this chapter, we have looked at the new strategic leader and discussed how systems thinking fundamentally changes the way the organization works and is led. Emerging from this discussion has been the concept of the organization as system. Let us look then in greater detail at the organization as system and understand what has historically held us back from its realization. In addition, we will look at its characteristics, how it differs from the traditional organization, the problems it solves, and its benefits.

References

1. Sun Tzu, *The Art of War* (Ixia Press, 2019).
2. Authors: A. Harrison, R. Bramson, S. Bramson, N. Parlette. The InQ is a proprietary assessment instrument, developed and marketed by InQ Materials, LLC, located in Palouse, WA, USA.
3. See research article: www.org-synergies.com/docs/I%20Think%20I%20am%20Therefore.pdf

3 The Organization as System

Introduction

I have argued that the strategic leader, influenced by systems thinking, sees the organization as a "whole." Further, she sees it as composed of parts that work together interdependently for the good of the "whole." In this chapter, we will start by looking at the traditional "siloed" organization and contrasting it with the systems organization. As part of this latter discussion, I will detail a number of factors that have kept the siloed organization strongly in place for so many years. Next, we will examine some "new age thinking" that has had some impact on the way that organizations work and are structured, but I submit that this change has been minimal. We will then look at my proposed organization as system and explore its characteristics and benefits. In this discussion, I will focus on perhaps its most salient system feature – namely, interdependence – and discuss some general ways that we can enable it. Lastly, we will look at the physical structure of the organizational system.

If we start with the worldview that many of our authors have described, we see that for almost the past 400 years, the Newtonian/Descartes machine model has prevailed. What has changed that view and brought us to our present day? In the first three decades of the past century, physics has discovered that the world is not exactly as Newton and Descartes saw it. This has led to the discoveries of quantum physics and the theory of relativity. Capra tied these discoveries in physics very closely to systems theory. They shared certain characteristics, such as the interaction and interdependence of components of the system.

In my book introduction, I mentioned that these changes have had a great impact on a number of disciplines, but have failed to significantly impact the corporate organization and the way it is structured and works. I mentioned also that some organizations have adopted a few systems principles in the way that they work and are structured, but I submit that it would be a challenge to find a contemporary organization that has fully adopted system theory principles, and therefore, truly operates as a system. But why is it necessary for an organization to operate as a system? What problems does it solve and why is it the best way to solve those problems?

Let us start our discussion by contrasting the siloed way of working with the systems way of working that I am proposing. How do they differ? And why does it matter?

If we start by looking at the traditional corporate organization, we see a number of functions such as sales, marketing, engineering, human resources (HR), operations and information technology (IT). Typically, the individuals within these functions share a corporate space and work closely together on a daily basis. There might be some interaction between functions, for example, engineering might meet with an assigned sales contingent to talk about future customer product needs, and human resources might meet with IT to discuss how they might help them with future employment needs. Many of these informal exchanges probably occur daily, but how might this change in the systems organization?

As I will discuss later, in the systems organization the functions may remain physically structured the same way. The difference will be that they will be more tightly bound together and driven by corporate priorities, rather than by their own functional priorities. We will see this in some of the examples that I will use from my consulting experiences – both the successful systems efforts and the unsuccessful ones.

One example is a client organization that wanted to develop a customer knowledge system. It was believed that developing this latter system would provide the company a competitive advantage by being able to more closely satisfy customer product needs. The traditional way to develop customer knowledge had been for engineering to talk to customers and to conduct an occasional customer survey. Occasionally, sales had also been consulted. In the proposed customer knowledge system, however, it was decided that people needed to work together across the many functions that actually interfaced with customers and, therefore, had important customer data that they could share. In the example that I am discussing, this would have been a systems way of working for this client – one in which people and groups worked together interdependently for the good of the corporation. Unfortunately, traditional functional distrust prevailed and the customer knowledge system "never got off the ground."

Inhibitors to the Organization as System

In general, we continue to hear criticism of our siloed organizations. Few argue for its merits. There seems to be a general consensus that companies would be better off if people and groups in the company worked together more effectively. Here, for example, is what Vijay Govindarajan, professor at Dartmouth College, said in a recent *Harvard Business Review* blog:

> When we ask executives, *What is the number one innovation killer at your company?* one of the first words we always hear, always, is "silos!".... Business silos, just like agricultural silos hold something important and make it hard to get at. That's good when you're protecting wheat and corn from rain and snow. But it's bad when you're trying to innovate across departments and divisions. And the bigger the company the more harmful role silos play. Silos create an environment where sharing and collaborating for anything other than one silo's special interest is virtually impossible.[1]

And there seems to be no opposition to the notion that it is good for people to be united in a shared purpose. As we will discuss later, we certainly see the latter in sports, military and musical organizations.

The argument of this book is built upon the assumption that it would be good for organizations to transition away from the functional silos of the past. But this is obviously not an easy thing to do. If it were, we would already have done it.

There are a number of things that hold us back from moving away from the siloed organization. I mentioned already the worldview of Newton/Descartes that has prevailed for hundreds of years. Also, we will talk later about the strong identification that people have with their functional groups. When asked what they do at their company, it is not uncommon for people to say that they are a salesperson, engineer, or they belong to some other functional entity. A third thing that holds us back from moving away from the silos of the past is our Western culture's emphasis on individualism. We identify strongly with individual achievement, as opposed to achievement that comes from working together as a member of a group. A fourth factor holding the silos in place is the metrics and rewards that are specific to the functions. For example, salespeople are rewarded for sales achievement; they are not measured or rewarded for helping the company, or another function, be successful.

Lastly, the "language" of the function is another element inhibiting our movement to the organization as system. We learn its subtleties and we become highly specialized. At times, it is difficult and unusual for us to understand and communicate with people in other functions. Information technology, for example, impacts literally every other function in the organization. We know that IT can have an impact on strategy, and we have learned that it has human, social and cultural impacts as well. But if we look at the respective functions responsible for these elements, we see that they have difficulty communicating effectively with one another. The IT person does not typically understand the human, social and cultural impacts of information technology – something the human resources person is vitally concerned with. And the IT person does not typically understand the *language* of strategy – something the senior management and strategic planning people consider very important. A Nobel Prize classic might dramatize this language problem between corporate functions.

Herman Hesse's Nobel Prize winning fictional novel, *The Glass Bead Game*,[2] may very well contain the secret to competitive success in the 21st century. Cast in a future period, one in which intelligent activity reached its fullest expression, the glass bead game provided a way for intellectual masters from various disciplines to synthesize their thinking into new planes of knowledge.

In appearance, the glass bead game resembled an abacus, with several dozen wires strung vertically and horizontally. Upon these wires were hung beads of various colors, sizes and shapes. Originally, as Hesse relates, the glass bead game was used by musicians as a way to build upon and improvise on musical themes. Moving these beads into new configurations symbolically represented the development of new, musical themes.

Later, the glass bead game was adopted by mathematicians. In this context, the beads corresponded to mathematical formulae, which were combined with the mathematical notations of other players, to form new insights. Over time, the glass bead game was adopted by all major disciplines with the beads corresponding to the symbols, formulae and notations of that respective discipline.

As the glass bead game developed over some 50 years, it became increasingly desirable to develop a common grammar and language which would transcend all disciplines and allow experts from these disciplines to interact, and hence, to learn from one another. In Herman Hesse's development of the narrative, this actually does occur, and now, we find the game being played with perhaps the introduction of a theme from astronomy, followed by a musical theme from Mozart, leading to the emergence of a whole new level of creativity and thought. The game continues in this latter form through the duration of the novel.

Picture the following hypothetical scenario:

Assembled in one room are executives from finance, human resources, legal, manufacturing, engineering, information systems and marketing. Each of them represents a highly specialized discipline with its own vocabulary, formulae and notations. As they play the "game," each person has a unique vantage point from which he or she contributes unique ideas and perspectives.

The game progresses as each player moves his or her bead in response to the movements of the other players. Suddenly, one player interjects that the ideas played thus far can be synthesized into a new strategy which embodies each of the ideas, yet transcends them. The players move on to a higher plateau of knowledge, delighted with the emergence of a new, competitive strategy which they all contributed to and which will make them successful in the years ahead.

Sadly, as we have discussed, this is not the scene in most organizations today. Either the disciplines do not speak a "common language," and/or they are not able to achieve an effective synthesis of ideas.

The glass bead game is a beautiful metaphor for the lessons from this book. We see individuals from different functions speaking a "common language" with which they bridge organizational divides, learn from one another, and create together innovative new ideas for the good of the corporation. The question remains, "How do we create this 'common language?' "

In the foregoing section, we have seen then some very strong reasons why it is very difficult to either narrow or eliminate the silos between functional groups. Let us now look at some of the attempts that have been tried in the recent past.

The Impact of "New Age" Thinking

If we take a historical look at the corporation, we see that a number of things have happened that, in addition to the changes brought on by the new physics, have had some impact on the way organizations work and are structured.

In the 1940s, as part of his doctoral dissertation, Harold Leavitt contrasted different ways of working and their resultant impact on task efficiency.[3] In a classic experiment, Harold organized two working groups – one that he called the "star" group, and another group that he called the "circle" group. Each group had five members, but communicated differently from the other group. In the "star" group, the individuals could only communicate through one designated person at the top of the hierarchy. In the "circle" group, individuals could communicate with individuals on either side of them.

After presenting each group with an identical problem, both groups equally arrived at the correct solution. When Harold next introduced a level of complexity, however, two-way communication became important, and the "star" group never did solve the problem. Harold's observations were that the "star" group was good at fast decision-making and control; whereas the "circle" group exhibited greater creativity, stronger adaptability when presented with differing conditions, and greater morale and enthusiasm of the workers. From Harold's experiment, we see the forerunner of our thinking today about organizational structure, organizational culture, and even network communications typologies. We know now that differing ways of structuring groups produce different effects.

In the 1950s, Digital Equipment Corporation (DEC), appears to have applied some of Harold Leavitt's thinking in creating a culture and a way of computer networking that were based upon peer-to-peer interactions between individuals. In the 1960s, something else was also happening. We were seeing a very strong value shift from the authority-centered days of the past, to a person-centered view. This affected everything from the way we raised our children to the way that companies work. Table 3.1 is a chart I have put together showing some of the elements of this transition.

In the early 1980s, the concept of corporate culture gained prominence. The first book I read on the subject was *Corporate Culture*,[4] by Deal and Kennedy, followed in the mid-1980s by Ed Schein's classic entitled *Organizational Culture and Leadership*.[5] What do we make of all this? Is the new way of working that we see in some organizations today the result of the physics shift, emergence of systems theory, the societal value shift, or the emergence of the concept of corporate culture? *Whether we would agree or not as to the best response, one thing is clear: the transition that Capra and others have*

Table 3.1 The Value Shift

	Authority	*Person*
Psychotherapy	Psychoanalysis	Client-Centered
Child Development	Parent-Centered	Child-Centered
Education	Teacher-Centered	Student-Centered
Organizations	Hierarchical	Networked
Computing	Mainframes	Client-Server
Computer Networks	Central Control	Peer-to-Peer

described, from the world as machine to a new worldview, is taking place in a variety of ways, but in my opinion, it is still incomplete.

Benefits of the Organization as System

Earlier, I mentioned that I would not be providing the readers a simple, "magical" answer to the question of how to best structure a company. I mentioned that there are many ways to do the latter, and some may be preferable depending upon the company environment, its history and other factors. I do believe strongly, however, that the systems solution that I am proposing is a very good one for contemporary companies. Summarizing a few of my arguments, it provides the following benefits:

- It truly optimizes the purpose for vertically-integrating enterprises. Enterprises were not created to serve as a jumble of independent parts that work for their own individual success.
- It draws upon significant and respected scientific findings. These findings have already made major impacts on fields such as economics, environmental science, biology, medicine and psychology.
- Like many of the "New Age" models, it is a participative model that draws upon the strength of the people in the organization. And like Harold Leavitt's "circle" model, I believe it also creates greater morale and enthusiasm among the workers. People enjoy working in these kinds of companies.
- It is unique with its emphasis on moving the whole system and its parts. As we will see, it accomplishes this with proven strategic processes that create and successfully execute desired long-term results. These results become the destination for the whole system as it moves.
- It is truly a total solution, with the benefits of a new systems way of working, plus strategic processes that create systemic identification of the parts with the "whole" and enable their successful coordination and integration.

Fundamentally, I believe the thing that differentiates the solution of this book from the "New Age" thinking that exists standalone in a number of organizations is my proposed use of the strategy processes. As I have suggested, I will use these processes to create identification of the parts of the organization with the "whole." More importantly, I will use the strategy processes to effect interdependence of the parts with one another, and the resulting integration of the parts into the "whole." An example from my consulting work might be appropriate at this time to elaborate on how the strategy processes can accomplish the aforementioned steps.

Several years ago, a senior sales executive from a client semiconductor company asked me to help him develop a sales strategy for the company. This involved a planning workshop with his senior team. In the workshop, we used a strategy tool that I will refer to again later in the section on strategy. This tool was called the value discipline and was based on research that showed that excellent companies tended to excel in one, and only one, of three different value disciplines – product leadership, operational excellence and customer intimacy; you needed to be good at the other two.

As a group, the sales team decided that customer intimacy was the value discipline that provided the company the greatest opportunity for success. Customer intimacy basically provided the company an intimate knowledge of customer needs. With this knowledge they could then uniquely customize products that addressed those needs and, as a result, gain an edge over their competition.

After the workshop, the sales executive presented the results to the CEO of the company. In the discussion with the CEO, the sales executive informed him that the group had chosen customer intimacy as their primary value discipline. He added that they needed to also be good at the other two. The CEO rejected this conclusion; he argued and firmly decided that the company needed to be excellent at all three.

Some weeks later, I met again with the sales executive and he proceeded to tell me about an interesting, recent, occurrence. He reminded me that the CEO had objected to having only one value discipline in which the company excelled. Continuing, the sales executive told me that one of their leading European customers had recently asked for technical support on a new product that the semiconductor company was developing. Because the product was very new, the only person that could address the customer's questions resided in the semiconductor company's engineering group. When sales requested the help of this individual, the executive in charge of engineering answered that he could not release him, because this individual's time was needed in order to make sure the new product was delivered on time.

The sales executive and I continued our discussion and we proceeded to analyze what had happened. The company had not been able to decide on customer intimacy as its primary value discipline, and as a result, when the conflict between customer intimacy and the operational excellence leaning of the engineering executive surfaced, the decision that needed to be made for the good of the customer and the company was not made.

This example highlights for us the main theme of this book. As we have argued, there is great potential for a company to operate as a system, enabled through a strategy process that leads different departments to interact with decisions that favor the good of the "whole." In the example I have cited, this did not happen. Without a clear strategy decision uniting the groups, we see decisions between departments defaulting to their departmental biases. We see also in this case the potential of the new form of strategic leadership described earlier by Russell Ackoff. As he said so well: "Supervision and command are the management of actions; coordination and integration are the management of interactions, and this requires leadership."

Lastly, our case example highlights an issue that we will discuss more fully later in the section on strategy. Strategy is all about choices, and we see here a failure of the CEO to make a choice that would have signaled to both sales and engineering the right thing to do in support of the good of the overall company. An interesting footnote to this case was the later acknowledgment by the CEO that he now recognized the need to have chosen only one primary value discipline. I was told by the sales executive that the CEO's comment was, "I would never admit it, but Pete was right."

Before leaving this section of the chapter, let me summarize what I have said about the organization as system. This book is about a new way of working and I have argued that a systems way of working is a very desirable one for an organization to adopt, given the complexity of the times and our displeasure with the organizational silos which tend to prevail in most organizations. Building upon the systemic features described by our authors in Chapter 1, following are the main features that I recommend for an organization to adopt in this new way of working.

- Organizational functions and subsystems working together collaboratively and interdependently to achieve a shared set of corporate long-term goals.
- An organization that is "open" to the environment of which it is a part and self-organizes in response to changes in that environment.
- "System Evolution" – An organization that learns, adapts and grows as a result of its interdependent interactions between inside groups and outside groups.
- Leadership that understands, and can effectively manage, the interactions between groups and directs the results of their interactions toward the good of the overall organization.

I believe the above features are doable in contemporary organizations; however, they do not happen naturally. In subsequent chapters, I will propose strategy processes and culture as enablers of the organization as system. Before I do this, let me first spend some additional time discussing what I believe is the main feature of a system – namely, its interdependence. It is this feature that will allow us to finally bridge the gap between organizational silos.

Interdependence

In this book, I am treating interdependence as the "sine qua non" of a system, i.e., that without which, it is not a system. Some organizations may wish to focus on creating interdependence between individuals and groups within their company, and even between their company and outside entities. We said earlier that in living systems, interdependence occurs naturally; companies need to create it. There is great benefit in doing so. Greater teamplay would result, we would eliminate many of the siloed functions in companies, people would work together more collaboratively, and knowledge and creativity would flow more freely between the previously separated functions. I believe that the foregoing benefits, by themselves, would make many companies more effective. *In my model, I have gone beyond interdependence as a standalone end to argue that greater organizational performance would result if interdependence served as a means to greater goal achievement for the corporation.* Having said this, I nonetheless believe that interdependence as an organizational quality is important enough to spend some additional time discussing how it can be enabled.

What Is Interdependence?

Webster defines interdependence as the "dependence of two or more things on each other." Dependence is further defined as follows: "A depending on another for material or emotional support (trust, reliance); a state of being contingent." One could interpret interdependence, therefore, as an inferior state; one in which individuals or groups are contingent upon one another. For our purposes, however, I would rather view it more positively. As with Hegel's dialectic philosophy, I view interdependence as the synthesis of independence and dependence. *I view it as the act of independent individuals (or groups) coming together in strength to pursue a common good which transcends their own, narrow, interests.* They are mutually dependent on one another for the achievement of this common good.

Is interdependence really a new organizational concept, or just an old one repackaged? Certainly, for decades, authors have discussed the need for integration in increasingly differentiated organizations. But integration is not the same as interdependence. For example, the vertical enterprise is integrated; the systems of the body are interdependent. We could say that all interdependent organisms are integrated, but not all integrated organisms are interdependent. There is a major difference between functions that merely work together and whose activity is coordinated, and functions that are vitally bound together in a common pursuit. It's the difference between functions being involved with one another in some form of coordinated activity, and functions being committed to one another's mutual success. *We know a lot about integrating functions, but very little about making them truly interdependent.*

Interdependence allows us to retain the best aspects of independence, while mediating the latter's self-centeredness and potential excess individualism. As mentioned, it accomplishes this through an emphasis on mutual dependence. It allows us, therefore, to be both independent and dependent at the same time. This latter concept corresponds well with Arthur Koestler's use of the term "holon," which Fritjof Capra introduced earlier. A "holon" describes a subsystem which is both whole and part.[6] As part, there is an integrative tendency to function as part of the whole, and as whole, an opposing tendency toward self-assertiveness.

Why Is Interdependence So Important?

One could look at athletic teams as examples of the power of interdependence. Individuals on football teams, for example, seek to excel in their particular area – offense, defense, specialty teams; however, as members of the school, university or professional team, they also compete for overall results. In this latter context, they are mutually dependent on one another for the overall success of the team. One could say, therefore, that interdependence contributes to competitive success.

The football example gives us another opportunity to examine the difference between integration and interdependence. You could say that the activity of football teams is integrated and coordinated; they all work together in some fashion. But there is a distinct difference between winning teams and losing teams. All things being equal, members of winning teams are passionately united in a pursuit which transcends their own narrow self-interest and the interest of their specialty group. It is this level of passionate commitment that we equate with truly interdependent organizations.

Another way to view the power of interdependence is by examining its presence in nature. For thousands of years, philosophers, cosmologists, astronomers, physicists, biologists and other scientists have pointed to the interdependence and unity in nature. An additional example of interdependence is the human body. For a discussion on the interdependence of the members of the body, we might, for example, go back two thousand years to I Corinthians and the writings of St. Paul.

> Now the body is not one member, it is many. If the foot should say, 'because I am not a hand, I do not belong to the body,' would it then no longer belong to the body? If the ear should say, 'because I am not an eye, I do not belong to the body,' would it then no longer belong to the body? If the body were all eye, what would happen to our hearing? If it were all ear, what would happen to our smelling? As it is, God has set each member of the body in the place he wanted it to be. If all the members were alike, where would the body be? There are, indeed, many different members, but one body. The eye cannot say to the hand, 'I do not need you,' any more than the head can say to the feet, 'I do not need you.' Even those members of the body which seem less important are in fact indispensable.[7]

If we were to summarize the above thoughts, we see that interdependence is important because it points all members of the organization to a higher, common good. Interdependence, therefore, would have us look at our activities in terms of what they contribute to the overall success of the corporation. According to Webster Robinson, in an April 1925 issue of the *Harvard Business Review*, the natural tendency, however, is not toward this greater good.

> There seems to be a natural tendency in every organism to jar apart and become a loose-jointed aggregation of unrelated units, unless there is some binding, supervising, and coordinating force that continually keeps them in place and makes each unit realize that it is not complete in itself, but merely a part whose greatest service is rendered when it fits perfectly into the whole.[8]

In the following chapter, we will discuss such a "coordinating force," as we discuss the role of the strategy processes. Perhaps, after almost a century, we will finally have a solution to the problem that Webster Robinson describes.

In this chapter, I have detailed the strong reasons for the continued stability of organizational silos and contrasted the latter with the benefits of an organizational system built upon interdependence. Chapters 4 and 5 will discuss the strategy processes as the main enablers of interdependence, but before we enter this latter discussion, it might be good to mention some additional methods that organizations might use to establish interdependence.

Other Enablers of Interdependence

I will use the following framework in several ways in this book. Built upon multiple sources and personally reformulated, I will use it here to show several miscellaneous enablers of interdependence in organizations.

As the above title suggests, the framework itself is truly a "system." Its components are tied together interdependently. A change in one element of the system impacts the resulting whole.

I will use the model in Figure 3.1 to describe how the strategic leader can enable greater organizational interdependence. While later I will discuss in depth the role that strategy processes and culture play in fostering interdependence, there are a number of other enablers of interdependence in the model that are valuable and deserve mention here. In some cases, for example, the reader will see people being brought together lower in the organization and will observe that strategic leadership does not have to happen exclusively at the top of the organization. I will say more about this very important point in Chapter 7. *Again, the argument is made in the following section that bringing people and groups together interdependently is a very good thing to do. Going beyond, as I have previously argued, to have them help in creating and reaching a shared destination is even better.*

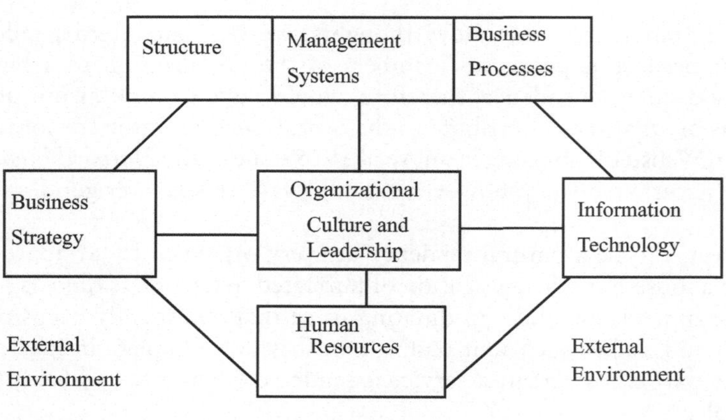

Figure 3.1 A "Whole Systems" View of Strategic Change.

1. Business Processes

Some years ago, there was substantial interest in business process reengineering (BPR). One way to use processes to build interdependence between functions is to create processes in which the members of the organization are parts of a much larger process, for example, customer engagement, instead of billing and accounts receivable. Indeed, that was the thrust in BPR – to build processes which crossed functional barriers. My own experience and the experience of others suggest, however, that these cross-functional processes are not always successful. There is too much power vested in our traditional functions, and redefining one's work can be a serious threat to this power base.

Another reason that BPR failed is that it became an end instead of a means. Companies targeted the cost reductions that process improvement offered them, instead of viewing processes as a means to help them accomplish their strategic objectives. When viewed in the latter way, the question becomes whether it would be more advantageous to redesign business processes to reduce cost, reduce time to market or to improve quality? Redesigning business processes becomes a strategy for achieving corporate goals.

A client of mine was one of the more extreme examples of a company over-emphasizing business process redesign. This client decided to restructure the entire company along the lines of business processes. They eliminated all of the traditional functions and departments, and instead, structured the company along the lines of five business processes. I can't remember all the individual processes, but remember that the effort was a failure. It eliminated the traditional silos in the company, but created great new problems with identification and accountability.

The idea of getting people to work on business processes that cross functional silos is a sound idea. As I mentioned, it failed because we made it an end versus a means, and we also didn't address the fear of loss that some experienced from the change. I believe that business process changes that result from strategic processes can be successful. If individuals see the changed work coming from a corporate direction that they have helped create, the chances of success are much greater.

In the chapter on strategy creation, I will discuss how great competitive advantage can be gained from bringing functions together in the Internal Assessment phase of the strategy creation process and having them look at activities that would tie them together. Previously, I discussed the case of a customer knowledge system and how it would have brought multi-functions together interdependently to develop custom products for the customer they serve. It is an example of reconceptualizing the product development process.

Another example of having groups reconceptualize their role in certain work processes comes from my work with IT organizations. Like many other functions, silos have traditionally existed even within this function; development, operations and relationship management have tended to see themselves as independent groups. In many consulting engagements, and in my IT seminars at Santa Clara University, I have challenged the groups to view themselves as

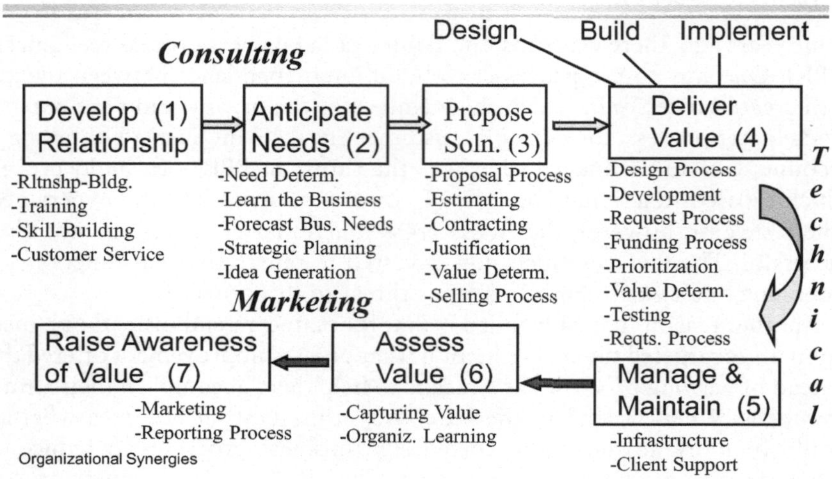

Figure 3.2 The Client Engagement Process.

members of a "client engagement process," instead of the unit to which they belonged. This process is shown in Figure 3.2.

In general, I have had great success with this approach. The IT organization of a very large telephone company, for example, began to see themselves very differently after our work together on the client engagement process. It is an example of what I suggested in my book introduction – namely, that the model I propose in this book can be used to bridge silos not only between functions, but also within functions and groups.

There is another interesting option for looking at business processes. With the emergence of interest in business process reengineering, we took pains to redesign the business processes from the industrial economy. A logical question to ask is, "*Why did we spend so much time and energy redesigning the processes from the industrial economy, when since the 1950s, we have been in the information economy?*" Shouldn't we have been devoting equal, if not more, time to the processes of the information economy? Let us briefly examine the implications of these questions.

Are the processes of the information economy different, and if so, what are they? A number of writers, such as Peter Drucker and Charles Handy, have maintained that the organization of the future must concern itself with knowledge. If that is indeed the case, then we will have seen a historical progression from data in the '60s and '70s, to information in the '80s, to knowledge in the '90s and the 21st century. What then are the associated knowledge processes from this shift?

Peter Drucker has said, "We now accept the fact that learning is a lifelong process of keeping abreast of change. And the most pressing task is to teach people how to learn." We could say, therefore, that the new work of the information economy is learning. The associated business processes would then deal with the creation, dissemination and maintenance of knowledge. If learning is the new work of the enterprise, then how do we bring people together to conduct this new work? With this question, we are brought back to the original theme of this book and see once again the importance of interdependence as a way to ensure that people work together to accomplish this new work. In effect, they work interdependently to learn from one another and to hopefully produce new insights for the corporation. At the same time, the process of corporate learning further reinforces their interdependence.

In recent decades, corporate learning has been seen as a source of competitive advantage. It has been argued that in our rapidly changing times, the only sustainable competitive advantage is to learn faster than your competition. Once again, we see the power of a new way of working, producing greater performance for the corporation. What remains to be discussed is how we create processes that bring people together to produce knowledge and creative insights for the company.

2. *Organizational Structure*

Another way to foster interdependence is through the organizational structure. In its simplest form, this means putting individuals and groups together in a variety of ways to accomplish assigned tasks. The "systemic organization," which I first described in the *Sloan Management Review*, might be an example of such a structural form.[9] I remember its origin was a presentation that a client had asked me to do about future organizational structures. I include it here to show the true power of a systemic organization. Not only would it work systemically, it would also be physically structured to support that way of working.

My purpose in including this organizational model in the book is merely to stimulate "outside the box" thinking about a complete systemic organization. The reader will see, for example, the unique roles that metrics, processes and subsystems play. While some may adopt aspects of these latter items, I do not expect that anyone will implement the complete systemic structure that I am outlining.

In the systemic organization, individuals are grouped by subsystem instead of by function. Essentially, the theory is that since systems are by definition interdependent, creating systems of individuals will by definition create interdependence among those individuals. Systems have other advantages as well. We can measure the efficiency of systems and detect deviations from the norm, before they affect the whole organism.

In the example of a manufacturing company with in-house production, we might see a manufacturing sub*system*, instead of a manufacturing function. Everyone who is a part of the manufacturing subsystem is concerned with the same goal of delighting customers. In this example, marketing would interface with customers and through that interface provide customer-centered input into the product development process. Engineering would design the products and manufacturing produce them. Purchasing would make sure that the materials are available to produce the products and distribution would be concerned with the flow of products to the customer. Service is of course concerned with the aftermarket results and providing superior service to the same customers. You might say that this is a system tuned to provide high customer satisfaction with all the members united in this common pursuit.

In a similar way, the other subsystems revolve around critical shared metrics. For example, the people subsystem might be concerned with the ultimate morale, well-being and productivity of the people in the organization. Using a biological metaphor, the financial subsystem corresponds to the nutrient producing aspects of the human organism. While it may not be intuitively obvious to make the sales organization part of the financial subsystem, it makes sense when we consider that sales is the main revenue producer in many organizations.

Next, we see the knowledge subsystem. Corresponding to the respiratory system in the body, we have a function that "breathes in" new ideas, information and knowledge. The "breathing-in" might come from inside the organization or outside. For example, the Internet and World Wide Web have become rich outside sources of ideas, information and knowledge. The challenge is to capture those elements that will truly benefit the organization, rather than merely entertain the individual users. Continuing the body metaphor, as with the circulatory system in the body, the ideas, information and knowledge are then circulated to members of the organizational body. In the process, some ideas and information are built upon and eventually become knowledge, while preexisting knowledge is disseminated as is.

Making possible the circulation of ideas, information and knowledge, enabling the conversion of some of these into other forms, and connecting people and organizations, is of course the electronic network. The knowledge system highlights this new value-added role of the information systems function.

3. Information Technology

The electronic network is currently seen as an instrument for building collaboration between people and groups. For our purposes, I would like to investigate further the role of the electronic network in going beyond this to foster interdependence.

I mentioned earlier Harold Leavitt's classic work with interpersonal networks. One of his conclusions was that the "star network," in which members of the interpersonal network communicated solely through one individual at the top of the hierarchy, fostered control. Borrowing from Leavitt's research, we have seen the control he mentions also in some electronic networks. "Authority-centered networks" (ones in which everything that is not expressly permitted is prohibited), tend to be controlling and hence limit the peer-to-peer interaction which is so necessary for creating interdependence. An example a few decades ago was IBM's Systems Network Architecture (SNA).

On the other hand, "person-centered networks" (ones in which everything that is not expressly prohibited is permitted), tend to empower people, and therefore serve as enablers to interdependence. As a result, they also contribute to organizational learning and knowledge creation. An example of this was Digital Equipment's Network Architecture (DNA).

It should also be noted that electronic networks can serve to isolate people from one another, rather than bring them closer together. A case in point is a seminar that I conducted while at Digital Equipment Corporation. The purpose of this seminar was to simulate the organization of the future. Accordingly, information technologies were used extensively throughout the program. For example, rather than face-to-face communication, members of this future corporation communicated electronically.

The seminar was very successful in showing the senior managers in attendance a new way of working, but we did have one very unexpected result. In previous seminars that we had conducted, significant camaraderie developed between the participants. This had been a major design element of these seminars, as it was of this one. When I asked one of the participants if he had gotten to know many people in the seminar, he responded that he had only gotten to know those individuals that were in his immediate small group. Inquiring further why widespread feelings of camaraderie had not developed, his response was, "Of course we never got to know one another very well; except for our initial introductory meeting, we never again met face-to-face."

The results of the subject seminar highlight for us one of the major challenges of our times. Even as we increasingly isolate workers from one another and increasingly use electronic media to replace our traditional face-to-face contact, we may be undermining our efforts to create strong bonds between people. And without these strong bonds, our chances of creating interdependence between these same people are hopeless.

Last year, I published a blog entitled, "We Are Losing Our Ability to Be in the Present Moment."[10] In the blog I described how we are losing intimacy with nature, ourselves and those we love. Our obsession with electronic media, such as smart phones, has distanced us in those interactions.

Along with the loss of intimacy I have described, information technologies are leading to the erosion of our capacity for concentration, contemplation and reflection. Nicholas Carr in his award-winning book, *The Shallows*,[11] describes the tendency to skim and his difficulty with concentration. In the following colorful quote, he writes: "Once I was a scuba diver in the sea of words. Now I zip along the surface like a guy on a Jet Ski."

There are many benefits to information technologies, but our contemporary obsession with them poses a challenge to the interdependence we have said would be desirable in helping us bridge organizational silos. Can we possibly be effective in working with others, for example, if we are not present to them? In order to build interdependence between individuals, we need relationships between them, and relationships are, in turn, built with people who listen actively to what we have to say.

4. Management Systems

Management systems are the measurements, rewards, incentives and controls that reinforce desired organizational behaviors. They also include the planning and budgeting systems. In the case of the latter systems, we see some of the factors that have contributed to our siloed organizations. If we first take budgeting systems, we see that budgets have typically been established by function or group, and then rolled up to create the corporate budget. We see in this process once again identification with the function, rather than the corporation. *What if budgets were allocated based upon a "return on value," i.e., the more your activities contribute to the corporate good, the bigger your budget?*

Our traditional planning systems further divide the functions, as each group typically establishes a plan based upon its own priorities, rather than those of the corporation. As I will outline later, having each function participate actively in the creation of the corporate plan is one way to make sure that the corporate priorities also become the functional priorities.

Earlier, we discussed the role of measurements and their power. In discussing the systemic organization, we used the example of all members of the manufacturing subsystem being measured on a common metric – namely, customer satisfaction or delight. In general, we can say that wherever possible, shared metrics would contribute to greater interdependence. This leads us to a fundamental principle in creating interdependence within organizations: *Whether it be work definition, or how individuals are measured, every effort should be made to define their activities holistically. Members of the organization should constantly be reminded that they are there to serve the greater good of the whole organization, not just the function or group that they represent.*

As with cultural change, what management pays attention to is also very critical in fostering interdependence. If it is clear to all that management really cares about people in the organization working together, this will go a long way toward successful implementation.

Some years ago, I consulted with a client who provides us yet another lesson on the relationship between management systems and interdependence. In this case, a highly empowered, entrepreneurial culture was held together by a strong family-like belief. As this organization grew large, senior management feared loss of control, and hence, became obsessed with the notion of "accountability." The combination of accountability and the continued belief in empowerment led this client to establish an internal market economy with accountability at the individual contributor level.

The results of these actions were instructive, to say the least. A preoccupation with individual metrics now prevailed, as individuals fought over who should get credit for certain revenues and who should get charged for certain costs, etc. In this particular case, accountability was certainly achieved, but at great expense to the previous family fabric and its associated, interdependent workings. This corporation, once one of the industrial stars of the 20th century, no longer exists – the victim of this and other moves that eroded the very things that had made them successful.

Another important element of the reinforcement mechanism is the control system. What does control mean in an interdependent organization? Historically, control has been identified with the autocratic policies of the authority-centered company. It is my strong belief, however, that organizations *cannot* function effectively without some control, discipline and authority.

It is certainly fair to say that much of the needed control will come from within the individuals themselves. This is the hallmark of an empowered organization. In this regard, the assumptions and values of the organizational culture will help the individuals internalize "what is right." And to the extent that the culture is a strong, shared one, this will be especially so.

It may be that control in the interdependent organization means that one controls systems, instead of people. As I discussed earlier with the systemic organization, by establishing metrics at the subsystem level, such as customer satisfaction, one can measure the efficiency of the subsystem itself and detect any deviation from this norm in advance of it affecting the entire organization. Perhaps that is where we should put our energies – to establish metrics that are holistic and can be shared, and then, to "control" to make sure that these metrics are achieved.

More work needs to be done in this area of management systems. For now, it appears that shared goals, what management pays attention to, appropriate control systems and overall consistency in behavior appear to be important elements in the interdependent organization.

5. Human Resources

I have not said much about the human resources and their role in creating interdependence. Perhaps it is obvious that they are central to any discussion and are the *subjects* of interdependence. Ultimately, it is they we measure and reward on interdependence, and that do the work of interdependence.

We could talk about the training and skills development that is necessary for interdependence to occur. Do our people have the necessary skills and attitude that it takes to be successfully interdependent? Later, in Chapter 5, I will discuss the *Wall Street Journal* article about the Army and their use of technology. It highlights the interdependence between technology and elements such as leadership and culture. Cases such as this could be used to educate people about whole systems thinking and the role of interdependence.

Related work has also been done in the area of teaming. Much more work needs to be done on extending what we have learned there to the organization at large. Another possibility is to recruit "interdependent-type" individuals into the corporation. These are individuals who have an affinity to work with others and who have a natural talent to "see the bigger picture."

As an example of a skill that might contribute to interdependence, one might mention collaboration. Here we could mention the role of social media and how it has brought together people from all over the world. While relationships have been established through this means, the question remains, however, how strong these resulting relationships truly are. Earlier I mentioned the example of the seminar I conducted for a group of senior executives that communicated almost exclusively via technology. The reader may recall that this resulted in a lessening of strong relationships that had previously occurred in this seminar format. Where possible, therefore, face-to-face collaboration remains as a stronger enabler of the underlying relationships that are essential for true interdependence.

Final Thoughts on Structuring the Organization as System

In this chapter I have discussed the organization as system, but have not yet described what that organization might look like. How will it compare to our present-day organizations? Will the transition to the systems organization be difficult?

I believe it would be very difficult to get away from our traditional, functional organizations. While they still operate like the machine model of old, there are clearly benefits to maintaining the specialized knowledge that they provide. The functions also house certain personalities. The sales type, for example, is very different from the financial type. And again, the HR person tends to be different from the engineering person. There is an implicit identification there that would be very difficult to break. *My suggestion, therefore, is to keep the functional groups and to modify the way they work and interact with other groups, and the way they interact with the "whole" of the enterprise.*

While keeping the functional organizations, there are other things we should keep in mind. A number of the authors that I quoted in Chapter 1 described stratified subsystems operating at levels below the "whole." This would lead us to view the functions as subsystems; for example, the sales subsystem, finance subsystem, etc. Viewed in this manner, they also correspond to Arthur Koestler's holon, an entity that is both a part of a larger whole, but also a whole onto itself.

Recently, I have both consulted and written about new organizational forms for the IT organization. In the process, I have been strongly influenced by the thinking about subsystems. The result has been the introduction of a position I named, "The General Manager of Strategic Resources." To this general manager position would report IT, HR and the corporate strategy function. In effect, this would bring the information resources and human resources, together with the strategic process of employing these resources, in support of the goals of the enterprise. It is a good example of a subsystem that operates both as a part of the whole, but also as a whole onto itself. It is also a good example of another way to structure the traditional functions.

I wrote about this concept, introduced it at a number of IT forums, and also discussed it with a number of IT organizations. To date, no IT organization has completely adopted the concept. While it has been favorably accepted by them, it is a good example of the difficulties of making organizational changes that affect multiple functions. It also speaks to the difficulty of making system changes, which by definition involve multiple functions and multiple levels of an organization. As we will see, the model I am proposing in this book seeks to address these difficulties by having all the people that will be affected by the system changes involved in the design and implementation of the system. I will outline this latter process when we discuss the role of strategy in the model.

References

1. Vijay Govindarajan, "The First Two Steps Toward Breaking Down Silos in Your Organization," *HBR Blog Network*, August 9, 2011.
2. Hermann Hesse, *The Glass Bead Game* (Bantam Books Edition, 1970).
3. Harold J. Leavitt, In: *Managerial Psychology*, Third Edition (University of Chicago Press, 1972), p. 191 ff.
4. Terrence E. Deal & Allan A. Kennedy, *Corporate Cultures* (Addison-Wesley, 1982).
5. Edgar H. Schein, *Organizational Culture and Leadership*, Third Edition (Jossey-Bass, 2004).
6. Arthur Koestler, *Janus* (Hutchinson, 1978).
7. St. Paul, I Corinthians 11:26.
8. Webster Robinson, *Harvard Business Review*, April 1925.
9. Peter S. DeLisi, "Lessons from the Steel Axe: Culture, Technology, and Organizational Change," *Sloan Management Review*, Fall 1990.
10. See: www.linkedin.com/pulse/we-losing-our-ability-present-moment-pete-delisi/
11. Nicholas Carr, *The Shallows* (W. W. Norton & Co., 2010).

4 Organizational Strategy

Introduction

We are about to begin our discussion of strategy and strategy processes. Before we begin, it might be good to summarize the main points from the previous chapters. In Chapter 1, we reviewed the contributions of five esteemed authors. In general, we heard them articulate the basics of General Systems Theory. They also argued that the siloed machine model did not address contemporary needs and, therefore, was obsolete.

In Chapter 2, I applied the thinking of the systems theory authors to the new role of the strategic leader. The resulting picture was a leader that viewed the organization as a whole, i.e. as a system, and saw the power of being able to move that system to a new, desirable, future destination. I argued that the most effective ways to accomplish this were strategically and culturally.

In Chapter 3, the organization as system was our primary focus. We looked at the factors that kept the siloed machine model in place for so many years. We also investigated further the essence of the organization as system – namely, its interdependence. Proceeding further, in addition to the strategy processes that we will describe in this chapter, we looked at additional ways that interdependence in the organization could be enabled.

Moving then from a summary of previous chapters, I have mentioned my experience over the past 30 years in helping client companies create a strategy for their organization. While in most of these cases the primary focus was on the strategy content, and not on interdependence per se, I have observed an unmistakable coming together of the parties involved in the strategy process. *The process itself of developing a business strategy can therefore be used to unite people in a greater cause, and thereby make them more interdependent.* Shortly, I will go in depth into the strategy processes and, among other things, detail how they accomplish this. But for now, since the argument of this book rests so strongly on the ability of strategy processes to create new, interdependent ways of working, let me start with a few examples from my consulting work where interdependence was either sought or was a byproduct of my efforts.

One example of interdependence being created was a major university that I assisted with the development of their five-year strategy. Universities are not well known for their ability to bring highly educated, independent disciplines together into anything resembling a common direction. With this particular university, however, the different colleges and disciplines came together over a period of many months, temporarily put aside the loyalty to their particular school, and built an exciting future direction for the "whole," i.e., the university. In the process, they invested themselves in a purpose greater than that of their individual school.

I have been involved in two inter-organizational situations whose purpose was to use the strategic planning process as a vehicle to achieve greater interdependence. One of these was with a large, domestic state. In this case, our plan was to use the strategic planning process to foster greater interdependence between the state government, the educational establishments and the business community. We theorized that if we could successfully create interdependence between these three separate entities, we would not only have established a successful model for this particular state, but indeed, have established a successful role model for the entire United States. Unfortunately, as the readers might guess, we were never able to get this effort off the ground. The very things we were trying to address – namely, bureaucracy and politics – got in the way.

The second situation involved a foreign alliance of ten independent companies. In the past, a loosely-coupled alliance had met the needs of all parties. Now, global competition made it imperative for these previously independent companies to band more closely together and explore areas of synergy. In this case, we used the strategic planning process to unite the parties in a broader purpose, and thereby, to foster greater interdependence at the alliance level. It should be noted that, at the same time, the individual companies continued to operate independently. *In other words, our design intent was to create strategic interdependence, while preserving operating independence.*

Another case example that deserves special mention, and highlights the power of strategy processes to effect interdependence, is the work that I did with several business partners of Digital Equipment Corporation (DEC). At the time, I had introduced a consulting practice into the company, and in addition to using this service to add value to customer efforts, we foresaw that the service might be used to make our partners more effective.

Over a period of approximately two years, I designed and led a number of strategic planning sessions with our key OEMs and distributors. The two-day process essentially consisted of taking the business strategies of the two respective organizations and, from them, developing a collaborative strategy to target the markets that we were jointly pursuing. Another unique feature of the planning workshop was an exploration of the respective culture of the two organizations and using this knowledge to mediate any possible conflicts that the cultures might pose for the collaborative strategy.

The program was highly successful and resulted in better working relationships between the participants in the workshops. In several cases, earlier hostile relationships between DEC and its partners were completely turned around. And in one case that I later heard about from the salesperson assigned to the account, the business partner in the year after the workshop achieved 125 percent of its quota.

My consulting exposure has provided me with a practical understanding of the limitations of strategic planning, as it is currently performed. These limitations come primarily from the lack of strategic knowledge among senior executives. Recently, I had a conversation about strategy with a former CEO. My question to him was, "Why don't CEOs make greater use of outside resources to help them with their strategy issues?" His response was that CEOs don't need outside help; strategy is what they do, and they are very good at it. He continued by saying that strategy is the CEO "sandbox" and they don't want "others playing in it."

Countering his response, I argued that many CEOs are brilliant strategic thinkers, able to think creatively about their products, customers, competition and markets. "What they don't know about strategy," I indicated, "is the way to translate that thinking into a process that makes the content of the strategy clear to everyone in the organization and makes it clear what their role is in that strategy." I continued, "They also don't understand the strategy execution process, the vernacular, the tools that practitioners use to surface the strategic choices that need to be made, and what contemporary strategy thought leaders are saying." I leave it to the reader to guess who came out on top in this debate, and if you guessed that the CEO didn't give up easily, you would be right.

Why don't senior-level executives have a better understanding of strategy? The simple answer is that almost no one comes up through a strategy function. Rather, they come up through functions such as finance, operations and engineering. The other answer is that universities do a good job of teaching the theory of strategy, but few academics have actually had the experience of having to implement a corporate strategy, and therefore do a poor job of teaching the *practical* aspects of strategy. As a result, senior executives rise to the top of corporations with only a casual understanding of strategy and the strategy processes.

Strategy Basics

Next, before I begin our discussion of the strategy processes, I would like to introduce a few strategy basics. I would like to define strategy, discuss its history, and most importantly, define the vernacular that is commonly used.

The Handbook of Strategic Expertise defines strategy as, "An approach to using resources within the constraint of a competitive environment in order to achieve a set of goals."[1] In other words, strategy is a means to achieving a goal. We sometimes also use strategy to refer to an organization's long-term direction. For example, "The company strategy is to…" In other words, when used in the latter way, strategy can include many items, such as mission, vision and goals. This can be confusing. In this book, I will try to be clear about whether I am using strategy as a means, or as the organization's total future direction.

The concept of strategy originated in the military. It goes back literally thousands of years to the work of Sun Tzu and others. Its origins in the business world date back to the 1960s, primarily with the work of General Electric. As a result of its short history, we continue to refine our thinking about strategy best practices.

Strategy Vernacular

In my strategy work, I have not had a senior executive team that hasn't asked me to define the terms we will be using in our strategic planning session. There is a tremendous amount of confusion about the strategy vernacular. Corporations tend to use the terms differently, and even in writings done by academics and consultants, there is strong disagreement on what the strategy terms mean and whether it really matters.

I will define how I use the strategy terms. In so doing, I will go to the original source for these definitions – namely, the military. It turns out that the business world has a limited history with strategy; it borrowed the concept from the military some 50 years ago. On the other hand, the military's history with strategy goes back thousands of years. In addition to my consulting experience, I spent six years as a military officer and will also draw upon that latter experience in defining the strategy terms.

Mission

The mission states the fundamental purpose of the organization. Why does it exist? An example I remember from my military experience was the mission of the Air Defense Command (ADC). Its mission was, "To protect the continental limits of the United States." In this example, we see that mission statements tell us what the organization does, and by implication, suggests what it does not do. For example, the ADC did not engage in foreign theaters. From the example we also see that mission statements do not have to be long. Frequently, I see mission statements that are pages long and include not only a statement of the organization's purpose, but also statements of values, stakeholders that will be served, desired organizational results and charters.

We see in the mission statement an excellent opportunity to apply systems theory principles. If the organization is indeed a system, then we should be able to express the purpose of this system in a statement. We should be able to somehow capture the interdependencies between the inside elements of the system and between the system and other systems on the outside. Clearly, this is not a simple challenge, but the process of trying to define the mission can itself be a valuable exercise as a company attempts to position itself as a systemic organization.

My mention above of the mission of the ADC is a good example of a systemic mission statement. In it we see how the parts of the ADC, such as operations, pilots, maintenance, etc., all come together interdependently to accomplish the fundamental purpose of the organization.

Vision

Vision is not a concept that originated with the military. It originated in the business world roughly in the 1960s. This was a time when psychologists were using vision processes to deal with phobias and other personal performance inadequacies. The process at the time consisted of people envisioning a very detailed, successful, future state, while in a very relaxed state. Its basis, according to Émile Coué,[2] was the belief that the mind cannot distinguish between something vividly imagined and reality. Its mental achievement served as psychological reinforcement for similar, future occurrences.

The business world adopted this concept and made it part of the strategy process. As currently used, a corporate vision is an aspiration of some future desired state. My instruction to my clients is usually along the lines of, "If all things were possible, what would your dream for the organization be three to five years from now?" The real value of either a vision statement, or as I will do, a set of vision statements, is that subsequent organizational goals will be loftier than they would be if the organization did not do visioning.

Goals

A goal is a desired, long-term, organizational result that will be achieved during the timeframe of the strategic plan. Usually, there are only a handful of organizational goals. In my work, the average has been four to six goals. The goals cover the desired results in areas such as financials, customers, employees, marketplace, competition and organizational development.

The most common error I see at this point is mistaking an organizational strategy as a goal. The goal is the end and the strategy, as we will shortly define it, is the means to achieve that end. "Whenever these are mixed up," I tell my clients, "organizational performance will always be suboptimal." A story I tell my clients that dramatizes this point comes from the 1988 Winter Olympics.

Some may recall that in those Olympics, Debbie Thomas, a United States figure skating singles champion, was favored for the gold medal. Debbie ended up barely winning the bronze medal for third place. While skating, she performed poorly on both of her triple axel maneuvers. After a slight miscue on her first triple axel jump, it seemed that her performance deteriorated and she ended up falling on the ice during her second attempt.

I watched the next morning as she was interviewed on television. During the interview, the interviewer observed that Debbie's performance seemed to have deteriorated after the first jump and asked Debbie if the miscue had bothered her. Visibly irritated, Debbie's response was, "Of course it bothered me. I went out to skate the performance of my life and after I missed the first jump, I could no longer skate the performance of my life." Watching the live interview in my hotel room in Seattle, all I could think of at the time was, "What if her goal had been to win the gold medal?" You see, skating the performance of her life was really a means, i.e., a strategy for winning the gold medal, not the goal. But as I have argued, when you confuse the two, your performance will always be less than it could be. In other words, your performance will be suboptimal.

I sometimes see a corporate goal that says, "We want to be innovative." But being innovative is really a means, i.e., a strategy, for accomplishing a greater result, such as growing revenues. When we make innovation a goal, instead of revenue growth for example, we might just be innovative in matters that don't really matter that much.

Another technique that I will use in my workshops to help the audience differentiate a goal from a strategy is as follows. I tell them that when you think that you finally have a goal instead of a strategy, ask yourself, "Why would you do that?" I proceed and tell them that if they can satisfactorily answer that question, they have a strategy and not a goal. In other words, they have a means for achieving a result that they have just elicited. And in almost all cases, the latter result will yield greater performance for the organization.

From the Debbie Thomas example, we could see that if we had asked, "Why would you want to skate the performance of your life?" a reasonable response would be that she wanted to skate the performance of her life in order to win the gold medal. The gold medal, therefore, was really the goal she should have been seeking.

Strategy

Classically, as I have already indicated, *strategy is a means to achieve a goal.* Strategies are usually limitless; a variety of means to achieve a goal can always be brainstormed by a given group. Once these are developed, of course, some will have greater impact on the goal than others. As a result, I will usually have my clients prioritize the resulting strategies in terms of those having the greatest impacts.

While strategy is a means to achieve a goal, we often use the term to refer to the organization's total direction. We talk about "the organization's strategy." When used in this manner, we include the results of our discussions about things like the mission, vision, goals and strategies. A very special challenge is deciding how to communicate the organization's strategy to employees and other stakeholders. What is it that we include and how do we make the communication simple and effective, so that they understand the strategy and their role in it? Corporate performance in this area has historically been very poor.

Objectives

An objective is a short-term desired result. Because it is short-term, it can be specific, time-targeted and measurable – unlike the goal which is more global. As with the goals, there usually are only a handful of objectives. If a goal is the desired result that the organization seeks in the three- to five-year timeframe, then the objective can be viewed as a milepost on the way to achieving the goal. For example, if our goal says that we want to be a billion-dollar corporation in three years, how big must we be by the end of the next 12 months?

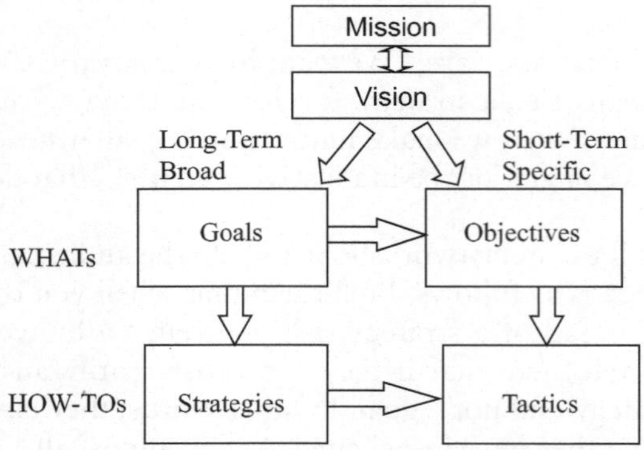

Figure 4.1 Strategy Vernacular.

Tactics

Tactics are the means to achieve the objectives. Therefore, they are also short-term and have greater specificity. Once again, we can look at the long-term strategies and ask what short-term tactics or actions we might take over the next year.

How do we pull all this together? We start by seeing that the strategy pieces truly are interconnected and interdependent. Next, we establish a clear definition of our mission. The vision can influence how we define our purpose for being, but should never exceed it in importance. In turn, vision statements give us lofty results to strive for in our goals and objectives. And the strategies and tactics now become the actions we will take to achieve our desired results. Doing the long-range thinking well makes the short-term thinking much easier and much more effective. Figure 4.1 shows these interdependencies.

Next, I will define strategy processes and detail how their actions and steps enhance the performance of the organizational system. I have argued that the strategy processes will enable us to create an identification of the parts with the "whole." As I will detail, this will occur with both the strategy creation process and the strategy execution process. I have also argued that the strategy processes will enable interdependence among the parts of the organization. This will occur as the corporate functions and groups come together in the strategy processes to put behind their own biases, and to focus instead on the overall well-being of the corporation.

The Strategy Creation Process

How does one create strategy in the systemic organization? Simply stated, the emphasis must be on the collaborative effort of the people to create desired, shared results for the organization. Later, the people and the groups within the company become means to help the organization achieve these desired results.

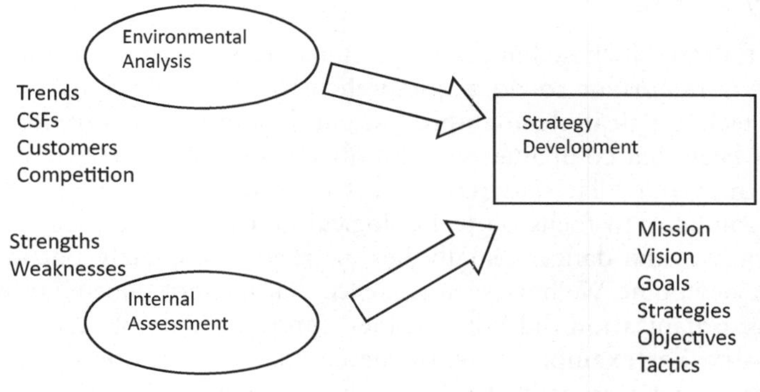

Figure 4.2 Strategic Planning Process.

In the systemic organization, the strategy creation process should involve everyone in the corporation. This differs from the traditional, strategic planning process in which top-level executives create the corporate plan and functional groups create their own plans. Some interaction might occur between the corporate plan and the functional plans, but the process does not usually take advantage of creative input from those below the top levels, and as we will see later, the process does not lead to the necessary understanding of the corporate strategy at lower levels that is so needed for successful execution.

While I am encouraging creative input from everyone in the organization, I believe the heart of the strategy creation process is a workshop session involving the CEO and her functional heads. I will describe this process in some detail, but first, let me provide an overview of the strategy creation process shown in Figure 4.2.

There is usually some pre-work that precedes the executive planning sessions that I conduct. Classically, work occurs on two segments that provide input eventually into the strategic choices that get made. These two segments are the Environmental Analysis and the Internal Assessment. These are highly analytical modules and the way they are done may not differ significantly within the systemic organization. Certainly, more emphasis can be given in the systemic organization to collaboration among all levels of employees and between functions. For example, some of the elements of the Environmental Analysis work could be assigned to subsystems, composed of individuals from *different* functions. In this manner, we begin to see how the coordination aspect of a system might be put in place.

In the Environmental Analysis, an organization takes a look at those factors outside the organization that will have an impact on the strategic choices that will be made. Here we will see a feature of systems that a number of our authors have previously mentioned – namely, "open systems." This is the quality of the system being open to its external environment and interacting with it.

Environmental Analysis

Items that are typically included in the Environmental Analysis are as follows:

Trends – It is important to do a comprehensive job of looking at economic, social, technological, demographic, scientific and business trends. My experience has been that companies will not always look at those trends that lie outside of their immediate environment. It is natural, for example, for a technological company to focus on technological and product trends, but as research has shown, the danger usually lies in trends completely outside of our immediate viewpoint. We have seen evidence that it is not unusual to have a trend that an organization did not consider important, completely disrupt an entire industry. For example, none of the companies that dominated the thriving ice-harvesting market in the 19th century converted to the refrigeration business. The Pony Express did not develop into a railroad. The producers of electromechanical calculators never made the technological leap into electronic computers.

Systems thinking provides us a new, valuable way to look at and analyze trends. As we have discussed, the emphasis in systems thinking is on the interactions of elements – not just on them as standalone entities. When we look at trends, therefore, we try to discern the patterns that have been formed between elements. Great competitive advantage can be gained through the use of this technique.

It might be appropriate here to say a few more words about systems thinking. While in this book I use "systems thinking," in the same manner as General Systems Theory, to refer to a broad body of knowledge about systems, here I would like to refer to its specific cognitive capability, i.e., the ability to discern patterns from a host of data. The research shows that senior executives tend to be systems thinkers and don't tend to get lost in detail. In our age that has put great emphasis on analytics, systems thinking is the ability to be able to abstract from the data and derive meaning from it.

A simple, somewhat humorous episode that I recently experienced might illustrate the power of systems thinking. One of my garage doors operates manually and frequently has been jamming. On two occasions, I have had to call a contractor to free up the door. On the most recent occurrence, the contractor came out and made a few adjustments to the door, but it continued to rub at various points of the frame. He continued to make adjustments, but every time he would eliminate one rub, another one would surface. He kept trying to explain to me that the door was old and there was only so much he could do with it. We both were getting very frustrated with the whole process.

Almost ready to give up, I happened to go outside, step back from the door, and take a look at it from a distance. It appeared to me that, somehow, the door as a whole needed to be moved. Reacting, I said to the contractor, "I'm not really a garage door man, and I don't want to tell you how to run your business, but it looks to me that what you need to do is rotate the whole door clockwise a few inches." With this, he gave me a rather strange look that I was unable to interpret, but he proceeded to go to a certain portion of the door and make another adjustment. He then tried to open and close the door again and it no longer rubbed, but flowed quite freely. As we have indicated, this is the power of systems thinking – to step back sometimes and look at the whole picture, instead of getting lost in the details. *The reader might also see in this situation an analogous example of the power of moving the "whole," as I have described with the organizational system.*

Another hypothetical case may further illustrate the quality of serious, business decisions that can arise from systems thinking. I previously mentioned my former employer, Digital Equipment Corporation. Imagine that DEC was doing a strategic planning session somewhere around the early 1970s. As part of the planning process, they would have been looking at trends that might have a critical impact on the company and its future. In those years, a major value shift was occurring from the authority-centered society of past years, to a person-centered society. In the chapter on the organization as system, I showed this transition.

Imagine that a participant in the strategic planning process might have called out this value shift and asked the assembled audience if it might somehow have an impact on Digital's future. To most, this would have seemed to be an irrelevant trend in those years, and of course, this questioning never happened. I believe if it had happened, systems thinking might have shown Digital that their future product strategy was going to be impacted in a major way by the realization that Digital was really in the "person-centered" computing business – not the minicomputer business. This would have made the person the center of the computing universe, instead of the organization, as had previously been the case. This would also very much have been consistent with its Chairman, Ken Olsen's, vision to bring computing closer to the user.

Discovering that Digital was in the "person-centered" computing business would not have been a trivial find. Subsequently, for example, Digital could have used this strategic identity to see a future that included personal computers and mobile devices – markets that they missed badly. Their inability to see this wasn't the total cause of its failure, but it certainly contributed to their ultimate demise.

We see here, then, the power of systems thinking and its ability to provide an organization a competitive advantage. For others, it may be a way for them to spot trends that could potentially threaten their future.

Customers – In this phase of the strategic planning process, the organization looks at what their potential customers need and value. Market segmentation can occur here as the organization looks at those segments that they will most likely target. Currently, there is a major emphasis on collecting data about customers and using analytics as a way to develop greater knowledge about those customers and their needs. Once again, systems theory would have us look at the resulting pattern, not just from electronic data that has been captured, but also from other customer interactions.

Working with a recent client, I helped him develop a customer knowledge system that came from the pattern that evolved, not just from electronic data that had been captured about the customer. More importantly, it reflected the result of face-to-face interactions that various personnel within their company had had with the customer. In this example, we see systems theory at work. My example highlights the interactions between different groups in the company, resulting in a pattern of knowledge about a customer. This pattern of knowledge was later used at the highest levels of the company to formulate both product and corporate strategies.

Competition – This portion of the Environmental Analysis typically looks at who are the current competitors and who they are likely to be. Once again, the patterns that develop, such as a number of new competitors evident in an emerging technology, may often be more valuable than the discrete data that identifies existing competitors and their strengths and weaknesses. We also continue to emphasize that the systemic organization is a participative and collaborative one. It draws its strength from the creative talents of many different people. Cross-functional subsystems might be used here, as well as in the other phases of the Environmental Analysis.

Several years ago, a client had me do an interview study of their major customers, partners and internal people. My client interface was a senior executive that had just recently joined the company and was interested in getting a quick snapshot of how the company was viewed by its stakeholders. My process consisted of mostly phone interviews. The exception was a written survey that I developed for the client's customers in Japan.

At the time of my interview study, my client was number two in their industry. They were closely behind their number one competitor. As a result, some of my questions dealt with how my client's company was seen vis-à-vis its main competitor.

I gathered much data over the ensuing months of the study, but most revealing was the pattern that emerged. Using the value discipline tool of Treacy and Wiersema,[3] I asked the individuals that I was interviewing where they saw both my client company and its competitor. I also asked whether, in the future, my client company could surpass its competitor by being a product leader, being operationally excellent, or by being customer intimate. The results were striking. The analysis revealed that both companies were excellent product leaders. In fact, they tended to leapfrog one another in different product generations, I was told. The survey also revealed that my client company was superior in operational excellence, but I knew that my client would not be willing to give up its high product margins in order to compete on operational excellence. Lastly, the survey revealed that customers considered customer intimacy to be the basis of competition for my client company. The latter was the positioning strategy that was chosen by my client company with great subsequent results. While my client company did not overtake its competitor, it narrowed the gap and produced significant corresponding growth.

Once again, we see in this example the power of systems thinking coupled with the strategy processes. The value discipline tool allowed me and the client company to focus on the pattern that was developed from the study. In my presentation of the study results and the subsequent presentations to other members of the client company, it was significantly more effective to highlight the resulting competitive pattern, rather than pages and pages of accompanying data. As we will see when we talk later about strategy execution, being able to communicate the strategy clearly to all stakeholders is a major element of successful strategy execution.

Market – What is it that our current markets value? Is this likely to change? What are the Critical Success Factors (CSFs), i.e., areas in which we must successfully perform in our markets? CSFs generally identify a number of areas that are critical to any organization's success in a given industry or market. Examples could be things like price, reputation, dealer network, product quality and cost.

Once again, it is critical that an organization does not ignore these signs for market success. A classic case that is often used is that of Toyota and its competition with the Big Three automobile manufacturers in Detroit. As the reader may remember, General Motors, Ford and Chrysler dominated the automobile industry for many years. At the time, it was believed that an automobile manufacturer competed on either cost *or* quality. Over time, Toyota's emphasis on the total system, which included both cost *and* quality, changed the competitive ground rules. The result was a major shift, with Toyota becoming the largest automobile manufacturer and the other big three manufacturers struggling ever since to reclaim their competitive advantage.

Internal Assessment

The internal assessment looks at the organization's strengths and weaknesses. Historically, many organizations have adopted the SWOT technique and added opportunities and threats to the strengths and weaknesses. Some contemporary thinking now argues that opportunities and threats should be derived from the trends.

If possible, this is another section of the strategic planning process that might benefit from group interaction. A technique that I use here is to first have the individuals in the group list the strengths of the organization on either a computer screen or a flipchart. I make no effort at this point to critique their contributions. On a separate flipchart, I will next have the group call out organizational weaknesses. When I am completed with these two items, I generally have two very full pages of material to work from. Later, in the strategy development section, I will discuss how I use the strengths and weaknesses to help the client develop a competitive strategy.

Group interaction to do the internal assessment could be another great opportunity to use the model I have introduced in this book. Shortly, I will discuss the executive planning session in which the functional heads come together for a multi-day session to make strategic choices about the future of the organization. Prior to this executive session, the functional heads might gather for a day to talk about their contribution to corporate success. Each function might present to the group their respective value proposition. In other words, how is it that each function provides a unique value to corporate success? The sales function, for example, might argue that its unique value is to sell the company products, and is therefore a unique source of corporate revenue. The foregoing could be a very interesting discussion, as each function presents what it perceives is its value-add to the corporation and lobbies to "paint a picture" of its function being the primary value provider in the corporation. Obviously, this would provide the latter function a greater share of corporate resources.

The group session is also an excellent opportunity to talk about the interaction between functions and how that affects the unique value that is delivered to the overall corporation. An example that I have discussed with many clients over the years, and also used in my sessions at Santa Clara University, is the example of the IT organization. In these sessions, I have challenged the audience to consider how the IT organization delivers its maximum value to the corporation. Historically, the IT organization has functioned as a service bureau that provides services to the other functions in the company. But is that the source of its maximum value to the company?

Contemporary thinking is that IT should serve as a strategic resource of the company. Instead of it being a service to the other functions, this argument says that IT delivers its maximum value when it helps the corporation achieve its long-term goals. While serving the other business functions is still important, this does not provide as much value as helping the company achieve goals, such as revenue growth, enhanced profit and greater market share.

We have just discussed a group session in which the functions look seriously at their value to the overall corporation and try to determine where the source of that maximum value might lie. As I mentioned, this occasion is also a great opportunity to look at the use of the model I am proposing in this book; accordingly, subsequent discussions might center on sources of value that might be derived from the functions working together interdependently. *If indeed unique value-add activities could be found that involve multiple functions, this would be a major source of competitive advantage because it would be difficult for competitors to copy.*

An example of functions working together interdependently to provide a unique competitive advantage is the customer knowledge system that I discussed previously. I proposed this latter approach to a client, which involved multiple functions coming together initially in order to arrive at detailed knowledge of their customers' needs. With this knowledge, the corporation would then be able to bring together multiple internal functions to design and build custom products to address these customer needs. As discussed, it would be very difficult for a competitor to match this capability.

It is important to underscore the foregoing example of the customer knowledge system and to emphasize that this is not the way that most organizations work today. Instead, we tend to see business functions acting alone through the stages of the product development cycle, and in the process losing the insights that would result from people coming together and bringing their individual ideas, perspectives and knowledge to the process.

Another possible element of the internal assessment discussion is "core competence," a concept that has arisen within the last two to three decades. In core competence analysis an organization looks at its root capabilities to determine if there might be areas that it can use to give them a competitive advantage. The power of this approach rests on being able to develop multiple levels of products from the core capability. An example that is often used is Honda. They used their core competence in engines, starting with small engines such as lawnmowers and portable generators, eventually moving to automobiles.

In addition to the Environmental Analysis and Internal Assessment, some organizations will also do Scenario Planning. The way that this is done is by having different groups within the company develop future narratives of what might happen to their company. With a recent client, I had one group develop a worst-case scenario, a second group develop a best-case scenario, and the third group develop what they considered to be a realistic scenario. After the groups had developed their respective scenario, I had each group present it to the executive group that was assembled. Each group was told that they should argue vigorously for their scenario to prevail.

The results were very interesting. In my opinion, the main benefit of doing scenario planning is the rich discussions that take place. Things are brought up that would never surface in normal day-by-day interactions. This later prepares the group for eventualities that might arise. For our purposes, we see scenario planning bringing groups together from many different functions and working together to arrive at a best solution for the corporation – a powerful example of the systems organization.

Next, let us look at the executive planning session that takes the data from the Environmental Analysis and the Internal Assessment, and uses them to inform the strategic choices that are going to be made. For our purposes, let us assume that the analysis that has been done before the executive session has been transmitted to the executive team and that some discussion has occurred. Let us move on then to the executive planning session, which constitutes the heart of the systemic planning process.

Executive Planning Session

This session should be attended by the CEO and all of the heads of the respective internal functions of the company. The latter will include functions such as engineering, marketing, finance, operations, sales, HR and IT. The purpose of the session will be to make the strategic choices for the company over the timeframe that has been selected. Historically, strategic timeframes were generally five to seven years. With the current complexity and rapid changes of the times, it is more common to see organizations paying attention to the short term and doing three-year strategic plans.

One of the byproducts of the executive planning session is the development of greater teamwork among the participants. Sessions that I have led have tended to follow certain interpersonal dynamics. It is not unusual, for example, to have the first day be somewhat conflict-ridden, as each participant "jockeys" for advantage. Often, one person's advantage is seen as a threat by others. To deal with this, I generally recommend that the teams stay together through the first night with a reception and dinner. This is usually a great time for the participants to work through the proceedings of the day. As well, it is not unusual for significant creativity to suddenly emerge among those present.

I was surprised, early in my strategic planning career, to see how the interpersonal dynamics changed from the first day to the second day. There would be an amazing amount of energy and enthusiasm displayed at the beginning of day two that was not present on day one. Also, relationships clearly appeared to be stronger. Over the years, I have come to expect these dynamics as part of the process.

There is clearly an advantage to having individuals engaged actively for a long period of time, working intensely and interdependently on the creation of a positive, shared future for the organization. The team-building aspect of the executive session is an important byproduct of this. We see in this example, then, the power of the strategy process to enable the interdependent workings of the organization as system.

The executive planning session, as I will describe further, focuses on the following major strategic elements. For a suggested agenda, see the Appendix.

- Environmental Analysis/Internal Assessment Discussion
- Mission
- Vision
- Goals
- Strategies

As I have mentioned, the analysis of the Environmental Analysis and Internal Assessment data should be presented to the executive team prior to the executive planning session. This, in turn, may prompt additional discussion at the executive workshop about the conclusions that the data suggested. For example, data from the preliminary analysis may have shown the presence of a new competitor. The executive team may decide this deserves discussion and subsequently places it in the "Competitive Strategy" portion of the planning agenda. Another more serious example might be a trend that basically suggests a possible disruption of the company's business model. This may lead to a discussion of the apparent threat under the "Mission" topic.

Most of the planning sessions that I have led have been with mature companies. As a result, they had previously been through strategic planning sessions and had developed some previous content. In my work with these companies, I tended not to spend a lot of time in the workshop on the mission and vision of the organization. My intent was to validate what they had previously done, and if necessary, to make some suggestions for how these two elements could be improved. Once I was comfortable with the mission and vision of the corporation, I turned my attention to helping them develop their long-term goals.

For organizations that need extensive work on their mission and vision, I suggest that they refer to my earlier definitions of these two elements and consider working separately on them prior to the executive session. Again, a group process might be used, with multiple corporate functions coming together to work on the mission and vision. This would further enable the interdependence between groups that I have emphasized in this book.

Goal Development

All the planning terms are important, but it is my belief that the goals are the most important elements of the strategic planning process for the systemic organization. It is here that we develop the shared results that we said were important for the members of the organization to identify with and to commit to; it is the desired destination to which we want to move the "whole." Without the goals being established as the destination that we want the organization to successfully achieve, it is very difficult to proceed any further in the strategic planning process. An example from my consulting practice might illustrate this difficulty.

I was once brought in by another consulting organization to help one of their clients develop an information technology strategic plan. This was a medium-sized bank in the western states. At the time, a relatively new CEO had been putting pressure on the IT organization to develop a strategic plan. The VP of IT and the Chief Operating Officer (COO) of the bank felt they needed outside help to accomplish this.

My process at the bank started with individual interviews of the senior executives, and also a review of their existing *business* strategic plan. *As I have previously stated, it makes no sense to develop a functional plan without first understanding how that plan would eventually support the overall plan of the corporation.*

In my interview with the CEO, he had proudly highlighted for me the bank's strategic direction. The latter was depicted on a colorful piece that hung on his office wall. It showed radii emanating from the center of the piece and colorful sectors created by the radii. On the sectors were written phrases describing the bank's strategy.

Generally, after I have conducted my interviews and done a review of the organization's strategic plan, I will summarize my observations with the executive team. In my session with the executive team, I was in the process of detailing my observations when the CEO asked me, "Pete, what did you think of our strategic plan?" My response was that the plan was elegantly stated on the colorful exhibit that I had seen. "It was obvious that you had spent a lot of time on it," I said. Continuing, I added, "There appears to be only one thing missing." "What is that?" asked the CEO. My carefully-worded response was that the strategy exhibit showed no goals. "The items written on various sectors were all strategies," I commented.

Visibly irritated, the CEO responded that I was not there to develop a business strategic plan for the bank, but rather, I had been asked to help them develop an IT strategic plan. My response was, "Sir, I cannot help you develop an IT strategic plan without bank goals that would serve as the results that we would want the IT strategic plan to help you achieve." Fortunately, in my defense, the COO voiced agreement with my argument.

Several weeks later, I returned to the bank and was greeted by the VP of IT with the following comment: "Pete, you won't believe what happened!" He proceeded to tell me that the CEO had taken the executive team off-site and they had developed a set of bank goals. "Not only that," he added, "the CEO has now agreed to be on our IT Steering Committee." For me, it turned out to be one of those rare occasions in which one takes a strong stand on something he or she believes in, and it turns out okay.

Returning to my goal development process in the executive planning session, Figure 4.3 is a slide that I use to define a goal.

It is not unusual to spend half a day developing the goals for the organization. My experience has been that we will usually end up with four to six goals at the completion of this section. We will have struggled through the possibility of 20+ items that are considered to be goals, and using the criteria that has been developed, we will narrow these down to a reasonable number. Figure 4.4 is a chart that I use that helps the audience realize that true goals fall into certain categories; the rest tends to be strategies and not goals.

As I have stated, the goals for the systemic organization identify the shared results that we as individuals and as members of various groups identify with and commit to achieve. In developing these goals, we take the functional heads outside of their comfort zone and place them into the role of helping them achieve these desired results. The functions become collaborators and means; we could say that they become strategic resources to help the organization achieve its goals.

- A "What" to be Achieved; an End; a Destination
- Usually Long-Term (3-5 years)
- Can be Global and General
- Limited Number (4-6?)
- Helps to Have Shared Understanding
- The Basis for Strategy
- When Done Well, Can be Powerful Motivators

Figure 4.3 Goals.

- Financial
- Customer
- Competition
- Market
- Regulatory
- People
- Culture
- Re-Invention/Transformation
- Developmental

Figure 4.4 Goal Categories.

At the conclusion of the goal exercise, the participants should have accomplished a major step in the transition to the organization as system. The functional heads should have begun to think about how their function uniquely helps the corporation achieve these goals. They should have also begun to see that it will require them working together in order to achieve the goals they have developed. Development of the subsequent means to achieve the goals will also highlight for the functional heads their interdependence.

Lastly, we should not leave this section without reminding the reader of the power of strategy to create a destination for the system that represents optimum performance. To accomplish this, in our discussion of the strategy vernacular we emphasized the importance of developing legitimate goals. We said that confusing a goal and a strategy would always produce suboptimum results; we would never get to the destination that we had intended.

Strategy Development

Once we have developed the goals for the organization, I lead the workshop participants to look at each goal and to determine how that goal will be achieved. The reader may remember the confusion with the use of the word "strategy." We indicated that, classically, strategy is defined as a means to achieve a goal, but in reality it is often used to refer to the overall direction of the enterprise. In this section we will use the word strategy in the classical sense as a means to achieve a goal.

In the strategy development phase, we encourage the participants to be creative and to question some of their assumptions. The group process enables creativity and it often comes in surprising ways. It also illustrates the systemic interactions between individuals from different functions.

Earlier I mentioned one of my early strategic planning sessions involving a company in the industrial chemicals and fertilizer space. In this example, I was fascinated with the power of the group to arrive at a number of possible information technology solutions that could help the Vice President of Mining reduce his extraction costs. One of the solutions, for example, involved using artificial intelligence to do more accurate predictions of the locations of the ore deposits.

Occasionally, I will lead the client organization to develop strategies in certain key areas, such as sales strategy, distribution strategy, product strategy and competitive strategy. For the development of the latter strategies, I will use a number of strategy tools. I have previously indicated that strategy is all about choices. The tools are powerful instruments in helping an audience surface tough choices. One of my favorite tools, for example, is the value discipline tool that was developed by Michael Treacy and Fred Wiersema.[4] It may be worthwhile to detail here some of the features of this particular strategy tool.

The value discipline model argues that excellent companies excel at one, *and only one*, value discipline. They enumerate the value disciplines as product leadership, operational excellence and customer intimacy. They go on to argue that the company must be good or achieve industry parity in the other two. In its use with executive audiences, I have never had a discussion shorter than half a day. In those sessions, executives will debate vigorously what they consider to be the company's current value discipline and the future value discipline in which the company should excel.

Summarizing Treacy and Wiersema's work briefly, the "product leader" is the innovator, the first to market with the latest and greatest technology or service. Time is their ultimate imperative. The "operationally excellent" company concentrates on the lowest overall cost of ownership for its customers. Here the emphasis is on quality customer service and includes solid, reliable products. Examples used by the authors were Wal-Mart, Southwest Airlines and Federal Express. The "customer intimate" company takes knowledge of the customer to the next level and is able to discern the needs of their customers so well that it can customize products and services into narrow customer segments. Amazon is a good example of this type of company.

My first use of this tool was with a large consumer products company. This engagement highlighted for me the division that occurs when a corporation does *not* have a shared business strategy. In this case, the Chief Information Officer of one of the operating companies asked me how an IT organization develops their strategy when their corporation either does not have a strategy, or it is not clear what it is. Having just recently been introduced to the value discipline tool, I commented, "Why don't you develop three IT strategies, each one corresponding to one of the three value disciplines?"

With this particular client, we used the Treacy/Wiersema model as the starting point for our strategy development efforts. It is important to note that the choice of a value discipline must be supported with a consistent operational model that converts it into execution.

In the absence of a clear corporate strategy, I first had the information technology function develop alternative scenarios for the three Treacy/Wiersema value disciplines. I did not know at the time what this would show us, if anything. I was amazed to see the incredible range of IT applications that would have to be developed if one did not have a clear sense of what the corporate focus was – a situation not unlike that in most corporations that I have worked with.

To further test the theory, I conducted an identical workshop for the manufacturing group at this corporation. In this case, I asked them to develop three alternative manufacturing responses, depending on which value discipline the corporation might choose as its primary focus. Once again, I was struck with the wide divergence among the three manufacturing alternatives. To develop the model further, we also developed three alternative operational model scenarios. A major shortcoming of Treacy's and Wiersema's work is that they discuss elements of a model, but never actually show one, or describe how to use it. For our purposes, I used the operational model which I described previously and which was shown in Figure 3.1.

These models, together with the previous work, showed quite graphically how the lack of a clear, shared strategy at the top of the organization results in functions interpreting differently what their response should be. And more

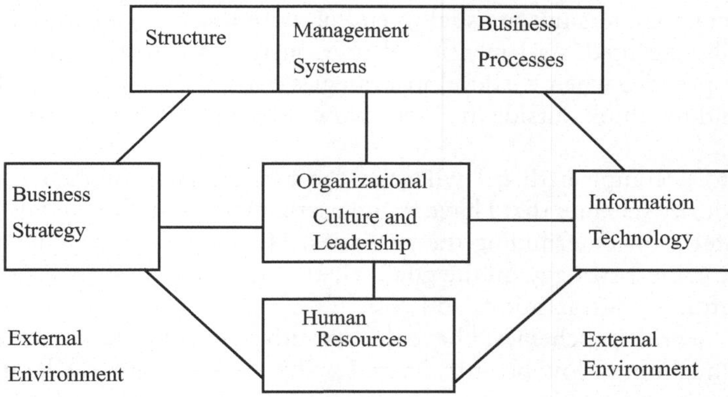

Figure 3.1 A "Whole Systems" View of Strategic Change.

critically, lack of a clear, shared strategy results in an inconsistent operational model. People get measured and rewarded for the wrong things, the wrong business processes are focused on, inadequate structures are in place, the IT systems support the wrong things, the culture doesn't match the strategy, etc.

Later, the CIO was asked to present her IT strategy to her boss, the CFO, and the COO of the company. In her presentation, the CIO briefly introduced the value discipline model to the two executives. I was in attendance at the meeting and was fascinated to see what subsequently happened. As part of her presentation, the CIO presented her IT projects for the next five years. She highlighted them on a slide that was filled from top to bottom and side to side with an overwhelming number of IT projects. At this point, the COO, looking somewhat puzzled, asked, "I don't get it; what is this all about?" Catching himself quickly, the COO replied, "I think I see what this is all about. You are telling us that if we are not clear about the business strategy of the company, you cannot be clear about your IT strategy." The CIO's response was, "Yes sir; that is exactly the point." The COO concluded with, "I would like to have you come and present that message to our Board."

My role with this client ended with helping them outline their next steps. The next step involved agreeing on a primary value discipline, developing a consistent operational model to support it, and communicating this clearly to everyone in the organization. In this manner the employees would be able to internalize the company strategy, and therefore, understand better how their work contributed to the success of this strategy. And the hope was that as people and functions lined up behind a common corporate strategy, their emphasis on the things that would help the corporation be successful would begin to bring them together into more of an interdependent fabric.

I would like now to leave my example and return to finalize my comments about the executive planning session. At the conclusion of the goals and strategy sections with the executives, we now will have developed a set of long-term shared results and the means to achieve them. When developing strategies for each individual goal, it is not unusual to end up with too many ideas that can be successfully executed. As I mentioned previously, brainstorming rules are very much in practice when we develop strategies and we encourage people to be creative and to "think outside the box." Now, it becomes a time to prioritize the best ideas.

In order to accomplish this, I will lead the executives through one of a number of priority schemes that I have found useful in the past. First, I will start by listing criteria for determining the priorities. The list will usually include: impact of the subject strategy on the goal, whether the strategy is realistic and feasible, timeframe considerations and cost.

In one of the priority schemes, I have the executives start by classifying each idea as high, medium or low priority. Next, I will have them rank the high priority strategies in order of importance from one through to the last of the high priority items.

By the time we have completed the prioritization of all our strategies, our two-day session is almost over. Prior to closing the planning process, I will spend some time talking about next steps – how do we complete the remaining objectives and tactics and develop actions to get us moving successfully onto the execution of the plan? Once the executive team has developed long-range goals and strategies in the workshop, it is not difficult in an off-line process to have people take the long-term shared results and translate them into results for the next 12 to 18 months. Again, in the systemic organization, this becomes a good time for collaboration and cross-functional work on these items.

Other Strategy Tools

In my strategy workshops, and at other times in my consulting work, I draw upon several strategy tools. The tools are powerful instruments for achieving the desired interdependence that I have encouraged. Previously I described, for example, how the value discipline tool can be used to get a group of senior individuals to debate and converge on one of three possible competitive positions for the company.

Strategy tools continue to be, in most cases, the exclusive province of strategy consultants and academics. Few corporate individuals either understand or utilize the bulk of strategy tools that are available. In addition to enabling interdependence between individuals and groups, these tools are powerful in accomplishing the following:

- We have said that strategy is all about choices; strategy tools help us focus the corporate strategy, so that the corporation doesn't end up trying to be all things to all people. The latter can be disastrous, as the company loses its singular strategic identity and confuses both its employees and customers in the process.
- Strategy tools help us clarify the corporate strategy, so that we can understand it, and therefore align our resources with it. We will see, for example,

how the use of the value discipline tool, and its related choices, brings a corporation to commit its resources in dramatically different ways.

- Strategy tools help us communicate the strategy to both internal employees and others. As we will discuss later in the strategy execution process, one of the causes of poor strategy execution is the lack of understanding among the employees of the corporation's strategy.
- Knowledge and use of strategy tools can provide a corporation a significant competitive advantage. Clarity about one's unique strategic identity can help a corporation more effectively position itself in the marketplace and provide it more effective use of its internal resources.

The use of strategy tools is a unique way to bring people together to work interdependently for the good of the "whole." We have discussed the value discipline tool. In total, there are approximately 14 different strategy tools that I may use in my consulting work. Of these, there are a few that stand out in my estimation, and that I believe would be of great value to those wishing to incorporate strategy tools into their planning processes. One of those I will discuss here is a tool that I use to help clients develop their competitive strategy.

This figure shows how a company or group can gain competitive advantage. The intent is to identify a number of strengths the company has that uniquely address needs that their customer has, and that differentiates them from competition. Figure 4.5 is a classical Venn Diagram.

In the internal assessment pre-work that I described earlier, one of the exercises that I mentioned had the client participants list their strengths and weaknesses. Returning to the strengths page that the group had created, I would now ask the individuals to identify the items on the list that they believe *uniquely* addressed the needs of their customer base. (In either pre-work, or previous market research, these customer needs would have been identified.)

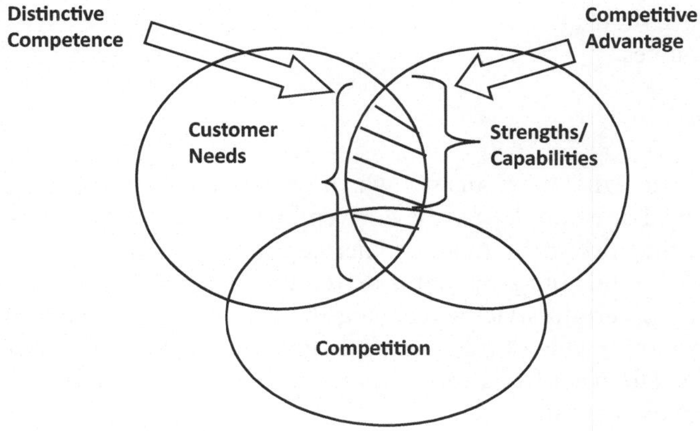

Figure 4.5 A Competitive Model.

The intersections between company strengths and customer needs are "distinctive competencies." From a page full of strengths, the group will generally identify only a small number of items that satisfy this criterion. Lastly, from the list of "distinctive competencies," I will ask the group to identify the items that exclude competition, and therefore provide them a competitive advantage. It is unusual at this point for the group to identify more than one or two items, out of a long list of possible candidates, that satisfy this criterion. Once again, we see here the power of a strategy tool to get people from different functions to put aside their own functional bias and to look at how they might work together with other functions to help position the company competitively.

Another tool that I will occasionally use to help clients position themselves is the "Driving Force."[5] Developed by Michel Robert, it is defined as follows:

> The one element or component of a business driving the organization toward certain products, markets and customers.

Michel states that the driving force is related to "Shepherd's Law of Economics," which states:

> Behind each corporation must be a singular force, or motive, that sets it apart from any other corporate structure and gives it its particular identity.

Following are the possible driving forces that Michel Robert suggests clients should evaluate.

A. Product/Service Concept
B. User/Customer Class
C. Market Type/Category
D. Production Capacity/Capability
E. Technology/Know-How
F. Sales/Marketing Method
G. Distribution Method
H. Natural Resources
I. Size/Growth
J. Return/Profit

Using the tool, participants must answer which of the above choices they are primarily driven by. For example, are they driven by their products or service? Alternatively, are they driven by the customer segments that they target and serve? Are they like an oil company that is driven by their production capabilities? Do they have a certain style of reaching the customer, such as door-to-door sales, for example? This should hopefully give the reader an idea of the driving force tool. The use of this tool requires more time than some of the other ones that I will mention.

The last tool I would like to introduce to the reader is one that I have developed as a result of some of the contemporary business trends – especially,

Product - Centered	**Knowledge - Centered**	**Innovation - Centered**
Product Knowledge	Application Knowledge	Customer Knowledge
Internal R & D	Knowledge Sharing	External Bus. Network
Technical Sell	Solution Sell	Collaborative Sell
Product Devel. Process	Knowledge Process	Innovation process
Technical Segmentation	Market Segmentation	Micro-Segmentation
Product Innovation	Service Innovation	Innovation with Customer
Technical Features	Innovative Comm.	Learning Relationships
Time to Market	Cross-Funct. Processes	Collaboration
Conc. Engr.	Knowledge Mgmnt.	Joint Planning
Organiz. Learning		Customer Relations Skills
Technical Degrees		Communication Skills

Figure 4.6 The Product, Knowledge, Innovation Matrix.

the current business interest in items such as innovation and collaboration. Figure 4.6 is an exhibit showing this tool that I have simply called, The Product, Knowledge, Innovation Matrix.

While the tool appears to be somewhat complex on the surface, it is a very powerful tool that captures the spirit of the times, and, once again, fosters serious strategy discussions between the different groups in the corporation. In turn, the discussions will help the participants to better understand not only some of the current strategic movements in industrial circles, but also to see that there is a striking pattern to these occurrences.

The tool basically shows the historical evolution of a number of business models. It can be used by a company to assess where they currently are and where they should be for best success. The product-centered model is one that I have seen often in the semiconductor companies that I have consulted with. Generally, they are concerned with getting the latest technology to market before their competition and their products involve a technical sale led by individuals in many cases with degrees in electrical engineering. Many semiconductor companies continue to remain in this product-centered space today. *I want to make the point here that a company can be successful in any of these three business models. It is important, however, for them to discuss the choices that these three models offer them and to decide which model is best based upon many factors, such as their market, their competition, existing capabilities, their culture, etc.*

The knowledge-centered model is one that product-centered companies often move to when their products either become commoditized, or are in danger of becoming commoditized. At this point, the knowledge-centered company will often inquire how their customers have been using their products. An example I will never forget is that of a company that produced explosives. I remember reading about this company; I believe the company was named Orca. The article related that Orca went to their major customer and asked them how they were using their explosives. The client responded that the explosives were used to blow up hillsides that contained a certain soil substance that the client would subsequently market. Inquiring further, the Orca salesperson was told that there were a number of factors that controlled the yield that was produced from the explosions. This initial inquiry with the customer led Orca to suggest to the client company that, if they were interested, they would provide a team of engineers to conduct a study of these factors that impacted the yield. The client accepted the offer and the study in turn led to a proposal to have the explosives company take over the explosions. In the proposal that they submitted, Orca said that they would be able to produce greater yield at a lower cost than what the client could do on their own. Needless to say, the client accepted the proposal. The foregoing example is one that highlights the knowledge-centered model. As I have indicated, it has been an attractive growth path for a number of companies whose main products have become commodities.

The remaining model in the exhibit highlights the innovation-centered approach. Here I have tried to package the current interest in innovation and collaboration into a more robust positioning strategy. As I have depicted, this strategy goes beyond the customer intimacy strategy that I discussed earlier. The company pursuing this strategy has gone beyond the product needs of their customer and is concerned with helping the customer innovate in other ways. The company salespeople have become more like consultants, and processes such as joint planning with the customer have become vehicles to understand client needs in more depth.

For our purposes, I believe the innovation-centered model offers a great opportunity to bridge functional silos and to enable a systems way of working, as I have described in this book. If we look closely at the innovation-centered model, we see that there is nothing that would predispose the company to offer their traditional solution to their customer. Products and services, for example, may not be the things that will best help their customer be successful. Perhaps, it is some unique form of knowledge that the company has that will help them. Reflecting upon this, I observe that a program that we instituted at Digital Equipment Corporation seems to have satisfied this latter requirement. At the time, our program to help our customers develop their IT strategy incorporated our technology knowledge, but greater value resulted from our knowledge of strategy, with which we helped the customer refine their own strategic knowledge.

I will leave the product, knowledge, innovation matrix here. There is much more I could say about it, but the main point that I wanted to communicate to the reader is that, once again, it is a tool that can be used to bring corporate individuals together to discuss contemporary business trends and to evaluate the matrix as a possible positioning strategy for the company. Whether or not the company chooses one of the options I have discussed, the more important benefit from using the tool is that individuals are leaving their comfort zone and working together to determine the best strategic alternative for their company.

References

1. Catherine Hayden, *The Handbook of Strategic Expertise* (The Free Press, 1986).
2. Émile Coué (1857–1926) was a French psychologist and pharmacist. He believed in the power of auto-suggestion and also maintained that the mind cannot distinguish between reality and something vividly imagined.
3. Michael Treacy & Fred Wiersema, *The Discipline of Market Leaders* (Addison-Wesley, 1995).
4. Ibid.
5. Michel Robert, *Strategy Pure and Simple* (McGraw-Hill, 1993).

5 Strategy Execution

In previous chapters, I have outlined the main theme of this book and described the new role of the strategic leader. Central to this new role is an organizational system which I have argued can best be influenced strategically and culturally. In the preceding chapter, we looked at strategy creation and described how people working together to develop the shared results for the organization is a major underpinning for the success of the organizational system. Now we will turn our attention to strategy execution. Without a successful approach in this phase, the dreams and aspirations that were previously developed by the organization will never reach fruition. Like so many strategic plans, they will remain on the shelf gathering dust. In this chapter we will look further at the critical role of the strategic leader in accomplishing this.

I cannot overemphasize the importance of this chapter. As I will discuss shortly, it is an area that has been badly neglected in the strategy literature. It is my hope that the strategic leader will use the tools of strategy execution that I describe to enhance organizational success.

Imagine a military or professional athletic team that goes into combat or competition spending less than an hour a month on its strategy and with only 5 percent of its members understanding its strategy. Imagine further that 92 percent of these organizations do not track the key performance indicators that tell them how well they are doing in the war or in competition. And finally, imagine that only 10 percent of their strategic initiatives are successfully executed. How much chance of winning the war or the championship would we give these teams? I'm sure we would respond that we would give them very little chance of winning. Yet, research that I conducted suggests that these are not fictitious numbers, but rather, actual corporate strategy statistics. Perhaps these numbers have since improved, but there continues to exist a casual perception that strategy execution is far from what it should be.

Some years ago, I undertook a major research effort to look at the strategy execution process. This research involved an extensive review of the literature, case studies from my strategy consulting and hands-on work with a client. The client work took place over a period of approximately nine months and involved developing, refining and validating the strategy execution model that I will propose in this book.

In reviewing the literature, my first surprise was that there was *not* a lot of material on the strategy execution process. Most of the material and most of the noted thinkers, such as Michael Porter, Gary Hamel and Clay Christiansen, put their emphasis on strategy creation, rather than strategy execution.

The second surprise was the number of interesting statistics that pointed to the failure of strategy in general. I remember, for example, one survey statistic that indicated that only 5 percent of employees understand their corporate strategy. Admittedly, these numbers are now old. Since I did the research, however, I have seen nothing that suggests that these numbers are no longer valid. As I mentioned earlier, the casual impression is that strategy execution is still less than what it should be. Little time continues to be spent on it, few authors write about it, and nowhere do you find strategy execution models or processes. For our purposes, therefore, I will assume that the sections that follow will provide significant value to an area of the business whose improvement offers great potential.

I continue to focus my efforts on ways to improve the strategy execution process. But as I will outline later, there is little hope to improve the hit rate on strategic initiatives until we bring the expertise of strategy practitioners together with the expertise of organizational development practitioners. Strategy execution fails from people, cultural and organizational causes, as well as from pure strategy causes. With over 30 years as a strategy consultant and 25 years of experience in organizational behavior, I feel uniquely qualified to attempt to reconcile these previously separate viewpoints.

Much more work needs to be done on this process. The model that I will propose represents new thinking, and as such, will need to be tested with many clients. Testing the model should involve tracking the hit rate of strategic initiatives over a multi-year period. This will not be an easy task. In the meantime, it seems to be intuitively obvious that we need to do something about the poor execution rate of strategic initiatives, and even small improvements resulting from the ideas suggested in this book will produce significant returns for companies.

The Reasons for the Failure of Strategy Execution

My earlier research outlined the following major reasons for the failure of strategy execution. Following is this material, updated with my more recent consulting experiences.

1. *Lack of knowledge of strategy and of the strategy processes.* In hundreds of strategy consulting engagements, I have found few senior teams who really have a solid grasp of strategy and of the strategy processes. The reason for this lack of knowledge is simple – few, if any, senior executives have come up through a strategy function. Not surprisingly, therefore, strategy oftentimes gets created, which is not strategy at all. No wonder the execution is also a failure.

2. *No commitment to the plan.* People were not involved in its creation. As a result, people don't "buy-in" to the plan and don't feel committed to it. Equally serious are the legitimate objections to the plan that are never voiced, because either the leaders don't create an open environment in which people feel safe, or the culture doesn't support it.
3. *The plan was not communicated effectively.* It is very difficult to communicate the strategy of an organization. Many make the mistake of communicating too much detail, while others do not communicate enough. It is also very difficult to know the most important elements that one should communicate. Lastly, communicating strategy in a way that people will remember is almost an impossible task. The latter requires some knowledge of communications psychology.
4. *People are not measured or rewarded for executing the plan.* Few companies tie compensation to the achievement of their strategic plan. It is safe to assume that the majority of companies tie compensation to financial attainment. At the time of my research, a study indicated that 97 percent of companies tied compensation to their financial plan results. Later, we will discuss how to tie the strategic plan to the corporate performance management system.
5. *The plan is too abstract; people can't relate it to their work.* People do not see if, or how, the strategic plan changes what they do. Alternatively, the plan is not translated into the short-term actions that employees need to take.
6. *People are not held accountable for execution.* Accountability is very different from responsibility. With accountability, people are held ultimately responsible for portions of the strategic plan and for predetermined results from that plan. Rewards and/or punishments are administered accordingly.
7. *Senior management does not pay attention to the plan.* We see this in cases where once the strategic plan has been created, senior management attention reverts to day-by-day business as usual. In change management dynamics, we find that "what management pays attention to" is one of the most powerful enablers of new initiatives.
8. *Strategy is not clear, focused and consistent.* As a result, people cannot understand the priorities of the business; anything seems to go. Also, they cannot "internalize" the strategy and act upon it.
9. *Conditions change making the plan, as conceived, obsolete.* No effort is made to update the strategy on a regular basis.
10. *The proper control systems are not in place to measure and track the execution of the strategy.* The organization also has no process in place to learn from the strategy and to update it as necessary. I will say more about this later.
11. *Reinforcers, such as culture, structure, processes, IT systems, management systems and human resource systems, are not considered, and/or act as inhibitors.* This is one of the major reasons for the failure of strategy

execution. In this regard, culture is especially critical. Each of these elements must align with the proposed strategy for the execution to be successful. Later, I will discuss a framework to accomplish this.

12. *People are driven by short-term results.* Short-term metrics, and the need to produce financial results for shareholders, drive people to focus on day-by-day tactics, rather than long-term strategy.

A Strategy Execution Model

In researching the few approaches to strategy execution that do exist, I found some good thinking. Historically, esteemed writers who have tackled the subject are Kaplan and Norton, Robert Simons, and Goold and Campbell. Each of them treated a piece of the strategy execution process, and treated it well. What is lacking, and what I therefore propose to address, is a *comprehensive* approach to strategy execution – one that addresses not only the management science portion of strategy execution, but also the people, cultural and organizational factors. With this latter approach, I will once again emphasize the importance of a systems way of working to bring these elements together.

There continues to be few writers who deal with the strategy execution problem. One book that received significant attention in recent years was *Execution: The Discipline of Getting Things Done.*[1] This book was written by Larry Bossidy, the former Chairman at Honeywell International, and Ram Charan, a noted management author, academic and consultant. While rich with their own personal observations, I found the book lacking a practical approach to strategy execution that others could use.

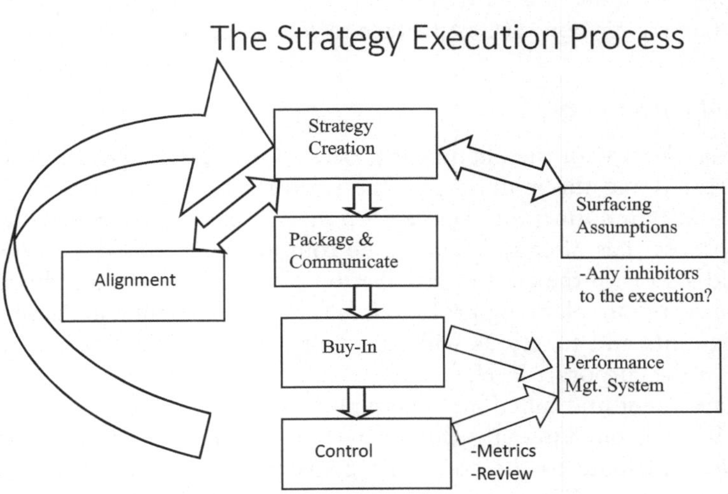

Figure 5.1 The Strategy Execution Process.

Figure 5.1 shows a model that I have developed to specifically address the causes of strategy execution failure. In the sections that follow, I will describe in detail each of the steps of this execution process.

Surfacing Assumptions and Objections to the Strategy

Once the senior team has developed the strategy, the next step is to ensure that no unexpressed barriers remain to the successful execution of the strategy. This can be accomplished in a number of ways. A simple way is for an objective facilitator to interview each member of the senior team individually. This facilitator can come from an internal group, such as Human Resources & Development (HRD), or be an outside consultant. The purpose of these interviews would be to surface any assumptions and objections, conscious or unconscious, that were not voiced in the group sessions. It is common for certain reservations and concerns not to be voiced in group settings. Politics, fear of risk, fear of being perceived as negative, and a variety of other reasons, may keep participants from voicing their full honest objections to the strategy.

Sample questions to be asked in these interviews are as follows:

- What are your feelings about the strategy that was developed?
- In your opinion, what will be needed to make it successful?
- What do you see as the barriers to its successful execution?
- Is there anything else you would have liked to see as part of the strategy?

Significant findings from this step should then be taken back to the senior team for resolution and the strategy updated with the results of the deliberations.

A less effective approach would be to anonymously solicit the same type of input in either an online or a written survey. This would not produce the same unsolicited comments, however, as the face-to-face interviews.

Alignment of the Strategy

The next step deals with the alignment process. Once the corporate strategy has been created and the inhibitors to the strategy surfaced and dealt with, the business units and functions can develop their own strategic plans. Ideally, this latter process has already begun as bottom-up input into the corporate strategy, and also with the active participation of the functional and business heads in the corporate planning process. It is now time to define in detail how the business units and functions will contribute to the goals that have been established at the corporate level.

The business unit and functional planning processes should begin with the question, "What is our internal value proposition?" In other words, how do we *uniquely* contribute to the corporate goals that have been established? A related question is, "What competencies and resources do we have at our disposal that could make a significant impact on the desired corporate results?" Once these questions have been satisfactorily addressed, the attention can turn to decomposing the corporate goals and the value proposition into individual goals and strategies for the business unit.

On the surface, the process I have described sounds very simple and straightforward. The problem is not that it is overly complex; rather, the problem is that many business units and functions have produced their own strategic plans without the alignment with the corporate strategy. When business units define their success independent of corporate success, the results for the company overall can only be suboptimal. *The reader will recognize that we have just stated one of the benefits of the organization as system. As we discussed in an earlier section, interaction with the other business units and the subsequent integration of the results of those interactions with corporate goals becomes one of the hallmarks of the organization as system.*

There are other aspects to the alignment step. In addition to aligning the business unit strategies with the corporate strategy, the "operations" of the business must also be aligned with the corporate strategy. In effect, what we are looking for is how each of the elements in the operational model are affected by a change in any one element. A change in the strategy, for example, will affect all the other elements in the model in some way. This is the nature of the systemic relationship that exists between the elements. Many strategies fail because their widespread impact on other parts of the business are not duly considered. Another source of failure is when the operational model does not align with the strategic choices that are made.

Figure 3.1 is a framework that I will use to show the interdependence of system elements in the alignment process. The reader will note that I have used this figure previously in our discussion of the organization as system. Originally, a version of this model was developed at the MIT Sloan School as part of their "Management in the 90s" research study. Based upon my own experience, I have modified the original model to show, among other things, a greater role for leadership and culture.

An example that highlights the power of the framework comes from a *Wall Street Journal* article.[2] While written some years ago, it continues to be an excellent example of interdependent activity. This article helps us to understand more clearly the contemporary challenge in our modern-day corporations. In a fascinating article on the Army and its use of battlefield technology, we glean insight into the interdependence between information technology, culture, strategy and leadership.

The subject article describes an Army tank commander in a simulated war exercise. As the article points out, "With just a glance at his computer screen, Lt. Devries had a better overview of the battlefield than any of the generals had during the 1991 Gulf War." Armed with this data, and seeing that high brush prevents him from getting a clear shot at the enemy, the Lt. asks for permission to move to a better position 500 yards away. His superiors refuse his request and the article goes on to relate the result.

> The lieutenant did as he was told, even though his computer and his own eyes had given him a better grasp than his bosses had of his odds of making

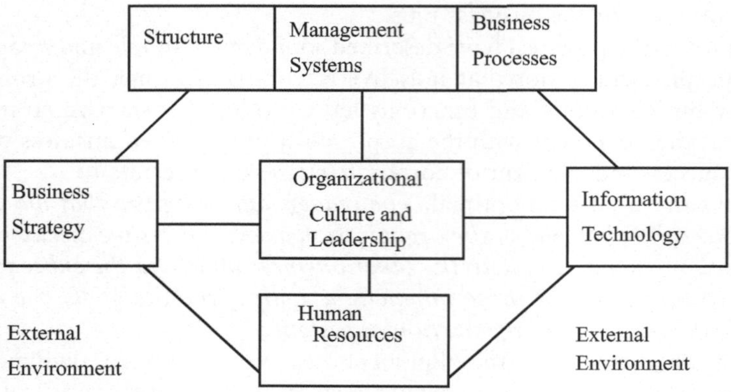

Figure 3.1 A "Whole Systems" View of Strategic Change.

> a difference in the unfolding battle. He fired off a couple of blind shots, but his efforts were wasted.

The article goes on to discuss the conflict between the traditional top-down, hierarchical culture of the Army and the empowerment that information technology permits. Leadership, and with it accountability, are also called into question, as one has to naturally ask whether a superior deferring to a tank commander armed with more data inverts the leadership pyramid, and with what long-term implications. For example, what if the superior defers to the tank commander and it turns out to be a tragic mistake – who is accountable, the superior or the tank commander?

The interdependence of strategic thinking appears quite prominently as well in the above scenario. As the author of the article points out, "One of the biggest challenges the Army faces is training troops in how to use all the data they have on hand. That means teaching them tactics and strategy, traditionally the province of colonels and above."

We have, then, in this short article an example of the leadership challenge in our modern-day corporations. Briefly summarized – information technology enables new ways of working and new levels of empowerment, but does the culture of the organization enable this behavior and is the leadership of the company willing to accept it? Additionally, how do we prepare the front-line troops with the strategic knowledge they need to operate with the information that they have? And how do we ensure that, armed with this new empowerment, they will act in the best interests of the enterprise?

What we have just read is a restatement and an enhancement of the main theme in this book. We see a new way of working enabled by information technology (instead of strategy processes), but still with the critical supporting presence of culture and leadership. As well, the article goes on to pose questions about some of the related dependencies of this systems way of working – items that perhaps we should equally consider in the model I have proposed.

Earlier, we discussed the use of the value discipline tool as a powerful way to get executives to make tough strategic choices in the strategy creation process. In their book, *The Discipline of Market Leaders*,[3] the authors of the value discipline tool state that the operational models to translate these respective value discipline choices into execution are different. A shortcoming of their book is that they never show an operational model. In my consulting work, I have used Figure 3.1 as an effective operational model that highlights the different value disciplines.

If we take this model and apply it to the respective value disciplines that we discussed earlier, we end up with three dramatically different exhibits, corresponding to a product leadership company, an operationally excellent company and a customer intimate company. These are shown in Figures 5.2, 5.3, and 5.4.

Viewing these exhibits, we begin to see the profound differences between the operational models of the three value disciplines. We also begin to appreciate how important choice is in the strategic process. *Failure to decide in the strategy creation phase how we will position ourselves results in a mixture of inconsistent operational elements by the time we get down to executing the strategy.*

If we examine each of the operational models closely, we observe that each major element of the model is different across the three value disciplines. For example, the culture that enables product leadership is different from the culture that enables operational excellence, and somewhat different from the culture that enables customer intimacy.

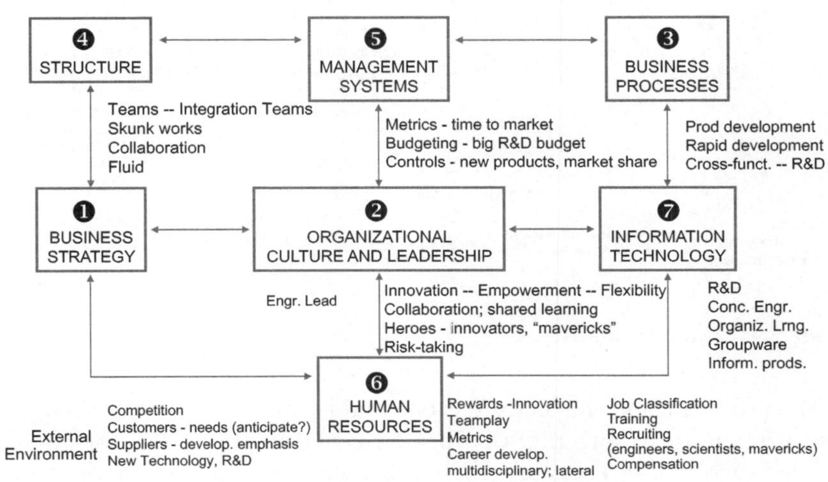

Figure 5.2 Product Leadership.

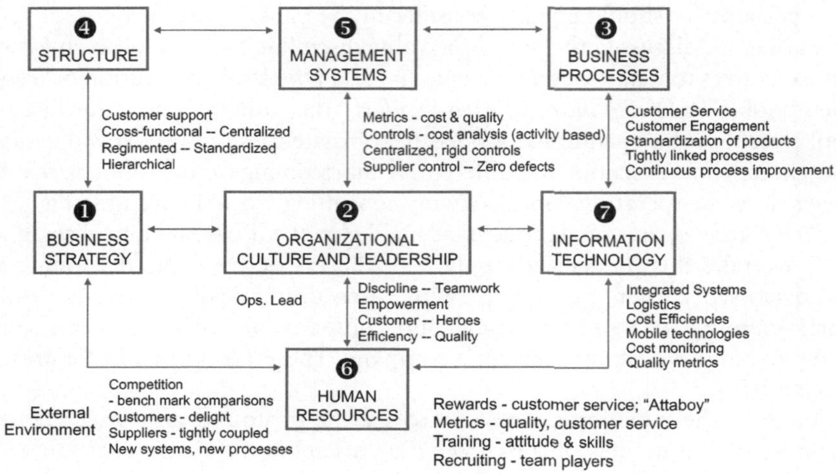

Figure 5.3 Operational Excellence.

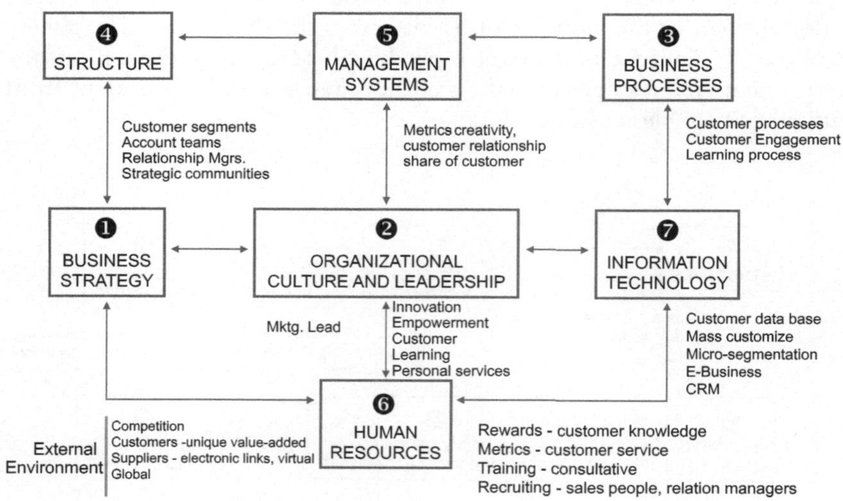

Figure 5.4 Customer Intimacy.

The product leadership culture is one that is empowered, risk-taking, entrepreneurial and can sometimes border on being maverick. One of my clients had just such a culture. I characterized their culture as irreverent, disrespectful and "off the wall." On the other hand, this company is the leader in its industry, having more revenue than all its competitors combined. So, a maverick culture can enable product leadership and the subsequent success of the company.

Examining the operationally excellent culture, we see that it varies greatly from the product leadership culture. This culture tends to be disciplined, less risk-taking, centralized and top-down. Since the operationally excellent company is driven by cost imperatives, efficiency and cost controls are very important.

An example from one of my consulting engagements highlights the strategy execution problem when an organization has difficulty making the necessary trade-offs between value disciplines. In this particular case, when I originally conducted the value discipline exercise with the executive team of this organization, they chose product leadership as their primary value discipline. At the time, they struggled, however, with operational excellence being a very close second.

I remember being somewhat skeptical about their initial choice of product leadership. In meetings with the CEO, I continued to debate the issue with him. I argued that while the product leadership company was first to market with new technologies and products, they often followed, rather than led, their competition in this category. I also argued that the company appeared to have more of an operational excellence culture. It stressed quality, cost and efficiency. My arguments were not successful with the CEO; he continued to argue that they were a product leadership company.

The value discipline debate with the CEO continued literally for a number of years. Each time we would meet, the subject seemed to come up and the CEO continued to insist that they were a product leadership company.

I don't remember when the change actually occurred, or the circumstances leading up to it. Perhaps repeated late to market launches of new products did it, but I can remember in a group executive session the CEO turning to me and saying, "Okay Pete, you win; we may not be a product leader company, but we want to be one." My response to him was, "We can work on that."

It is sometimes very difficult to move a company from one value discipline to another. In the aforementioned example, the transition was not easy to move from being operationally excellent to being a product leader, but since they had strong elements of both, they were able to accomplish it.

In another example, we could argue that part of Digital Equipment Corporation's failure was the result of the inherent difficulty of moving their culture from an innovative, empowered, product leader culture to a more disciplined, efficient, operationally excellent culture. The latter became necessary when Digital hired 26,800 people in two years to go head-to-head with IBM and the anticipated growth did not occur.[4]

The exhibits shown highlight the importance of the alignment step in the strategy process. We begin to see that not only is it necessary to conduct this step, but also, we begin to see, as we have said, how the choices in the strategy creation step have profound implications for the subsequent steps. If the strategic choices are not made in the strategy creation step, much confusion throughout the company and on the part of customers is the result. In addition, employees throughout the company are forced to make the choices day-by-day, without any guidance as to which choice will have the greatest impact on the company's success. As William Giles says,

> The front line of the organization, when left to the ambiguities of interpreting weak strategy on their own, often find little to implement at all…and the organization may actually move in the wrong direction as opposed to no direction at all.[5]

In this book, I have continued to stress how important the strategy processes are in the model that I have proposed. In this recent section on alignment of the strategy, we see again the clarity that first results from people working together interdependently to define who they are and where they are going. Later, this clarity is important in arriving at the desired destination.

Packaging and Communicating the Strategy

Once the strategy has been created, assumptions and objections checked with the participants, and the strategy aligned with the operational models, we can begin to package and communicate the strategy to *all* the people in the organization. I remember statistics from my earlier research indicating that the typical company gives plan access to only 42 percent of managers and 27 percent of employees. Again, how can we expect employees to be strategic, when they do not even have knowledge of the strategy?

To effectively mobilize everyone in the organization, the strategy must be clear. Theodore Levitt, the late, esteemed, marketing guru from the Harvard Business School, said it quite well.

> To be successful a strategy must also be simple, clear and expressible in only a few written lines. If it is elaborate and complex, and takes a lot of space or time to communicate, few people will understand it or march to its tune.[6]

The challenge then becomes, how does one successfully package a strategy? From my previous marketing experience at Digital Equipment Corporation, I know that symbolic representation can be a powerful way to communicate strategy. We know how much more powerful images are in communication. For example, the right hemisphere of the brain, used in processing images, can reproduce the image of a face long after the person has left one's presence. Imagine trying to describe that same face with detailed text. By the time we would finish our description of the many prominent features of one's face, we would have lost the essence of the visual image.

A simple image that I used in my marketing days is shown in Figure 5.5. It was used to communicate to everyone in the company the markets that we were pursuing, the applications that we were selling into those market segments and the corresponding product or service that addressed the application and that market segment. The message was simple, "This is our strategy. If it isn't on this cube, don't waste your time pursuing it." In a similar way, companies could use this or other symbolic representations to depict their business strategy.

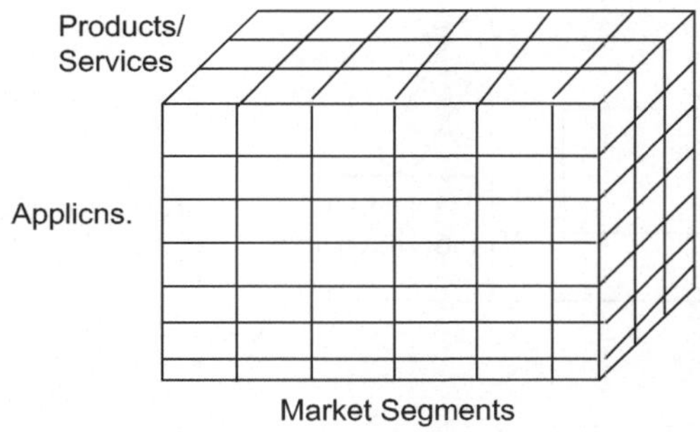

Figure 5.5 Market Segmentation Cube.

There are other ways to depict strategy. One of the best examples that I continue to use is that developed by the strategy consultant, Michel Robert. Michel used the principal of "driving force," as I described in Chapter 4, to capture a fundamental aspect of each company's business.[7] Following are two of his examples from a product-driven business, and secondly, from a technology or know-how driven company. From these you see the tremendous power of being able to express the strategy in only a few written lines.

> Our strategy is to provide and support industry standard, real-time *computer systems* for *time critical* applications that require high I/0 throughput and fast, predictable interrupt responses. We will do this in high potential industry segments that we can dominate with added-value, differentiated, reliable products, services, and tools that are easily configurable and can be tailored to meet the specific needs of these applications. We would do this in geographic areas where we can achieve enough critical mass to justify adequate support.
>
> Our strategy will be to seek and exploit applications for *digital signal acquisition*, processing, and presentation technologies and provide data analysis solutions that enhance the productivity of users. We will respond with high-quality, differentiated products, services, and/or systems that bring added value and provide a substantial competitive advantage. We will do this primarily in selected worldwide nonconsumer market segments that can be serviced and supported.

Achieving Buy-In

We indicated earlier that some of the causes of strategy failure arise from a lack of understanding of the strategy, the inability of employees to translate the strategy into their day-by-day job, and from the feeling that they were not involved in the creation of the plan. This results in a lack of employee "buy-in" or commitment. There are a number of ways to address these concerns.

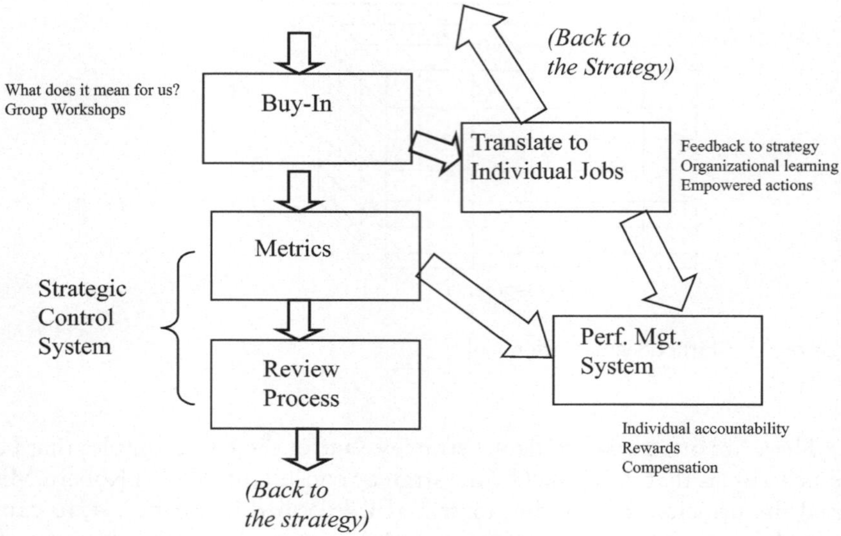

Figure 5.6 Strategy Execution Process.
Note: The Buy-In and Control Processes in More Detail.

The solution I recommend with my clients is that each level meets with his/her direct reports in a half-day working format. Figure 5.6 shows this process.

In this meeting the primary questions to be discussed are:

- How do the corporate strategy and our own business unit strategy affect the work that we do?
- How will they affect the work that we do with other corporate groups?
- What will change in our area as a result of the strategies?
- What reservations do we have about the strategies? How would you propose to rectify these shortcomings?
- How will we plan to support the subject strategies? What specific actions will we take?

We see here once again a strategy process enabling a systems way of working. Previously we saw the strategy creation process accomplishing this. Now, we turn our attention to the strategy execution process. In the group working session, people are brought together to discuss how their work will contribute to the overall success of the corporation.

For effective buy-in to be accomplished, there also must be a feedback loop from these sessions back up to senior management. People must feel they have a say in influencing the corporate strategy. Indeed, their ideas oftentimes represent unique points of view and are, therefore, quite valuable.

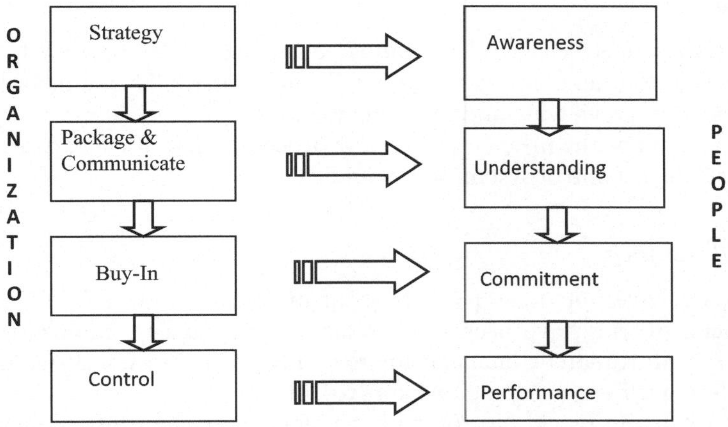

Figure 5.7 Combining Strategy Execution and Change Management.

Another way to view the strategy execution process is by analyzing what happens to people during the process. Figure 5.7 shows this quite dramatically.

I have just described the commitment or "buy-in" necessary for successful strategy execution. The above figure shows additional stages that people experience. Each stage corresponds to an activity that is simultaneously going on in the strategy execution process. For example, as the strategy is being created, it is not unusual for other people in the organization to be *aware* that this activity is going on and to have some anxiety about it. It is not until the strategy is successfully packaged and communicated to everyone, however, that some level of *understanding* occurs.

The next stage, as I have described, is the *commitment* stage. People not only understand the strategy, they understand their role in it and feel committed to do their part in its successful implementation.

The last stage, and perhaps the most important, is the *performance* stage. In the final analysis, success in the three preceding stages without performance must still be considered a failure overall. Performance is where we achieve the intended results for the organization. In this stage, control systems ensure that people are measured, tracked and rewarded for the desired results. In the following section, I will discuss how to accomplish this latter step.

We see from Figure 5.7 the source of many strategy failures. While some strategy practitioners have focused on the strategy execution process, in general, they have not had the organizational development (OD) and HR knowledge to adequately address the related people issues. On the other hand, the OD consultants and HR practitioners have, in general, not had the strategy knowledge to adequately address issues with the strategy process. One without the other is a sure recipe for failure.

Strategic Control

Once the strategy has been created, validated, aligned, communicated, and buy-in achieved, the next step is to "control" the strategy. This control step includes measuring, reviewing and updating the strategy.

First, let us look at the metrics and review processes that, for me, form the core of the strategic control system in my model.

Measuring the Strategy

In the past, we have not done a good job of measuring strategy. For many years, financial metrics have been the primary way to assess organizational performance. Unfortunately, financial metrics only tell us how well we have done – *not* how well we are doing or likely to do.

Robert Kaplan and David Norton have revolutionized the study of metrics with their introduction of the "balanced scorecard."[8] The balanced scorecard continues to be popular and includes financial metrics, but in addition, includes a customer perspective, internal business perspective and innovation and learning perspective. The customer perspective addresses how customers see you, while the internal business perspective addresses what we must excel at. The innovation and learning perspective exhorts us to continue to improve and create value.

Kaplan and Norton later attempted to map their balanced scorecard to organizational strategy.[9] In the process, they have done a masterful job of tying together items, such as goals, customer value propositions and performance metrics. In terms of a comprehensive strategy execution model, however, what is again missing is any attempt to specifically deal with the major causes of strategy execution failure – namely, the people, cultural and organizational issues.

If we look at the causes of strategy execution failure again, Kaplan and Norton do a good job of addressing item #11, particularly the alignment of the strategy with the business processes and the metrics. Noticeably absent, however, is any recognition that despite our best efforts to align performance metrics with strategy, the culture, as in the example of Digital Equipment Corporation that I have mentioned, may unseat our best efforts.

If we continue with our discussion of metrics, there are a number of things we can do in this area. Borrowing from Kaplan and Norton, the first thing is:

METRICS NEED TO BE BALANCED AND INCLUDE MORE THAN FINANCIAL METRICS

Following are other recommendations that have emerged from my consulting work:

METRICS SHOULD CAPTURE BOTH OPERATIONAL AND STRATEGIC MEASURES

Once again, too much emphasis in the past has been on operational metrics, as opposed to strategic metrics. Rare is the company that measures both.

Operational metrics, such as budgets and progress reports, need to be continued, but strategic metrics need to be added. These include monitoring of major milestones and progress against key success factors.

METRICS NEED TO BE BIASED

Metrics should be tailored to company priorities, should be dictated by strategic objectives, and should focus on the main challenges and the key differentiators for their products and services. For example, using once again the Michael Treacy/Fred Wiersema value discipline model, if one has decided to be a product leader, then metrics should include items such as market share, cycle time and number of new products introduced during a given time.

METRICS SHOULD BE TAILORED TO THE STAGE OF THE BUSINESS

Organizations go through various stages, and depending on these stages, different things are important. For example, during the early stages of growth, items such as revenue growth, market share and new customer acquisition are very important. As the business matures, costs and efficiency measures become increasingly more important. The dot com experience has taught us that profit is important at *every* stage of the business.

INDIVIDUAL METRICS SHOULD BE INCLUDED AND ALIGNED WITH CORPORATE METRICS

An ideal way to translate corporate strategy into individual performance is through the system of metrics. Once the linkage is established between the corporate strategy and the work of departments and individuals, the next step is to assign metrics to the results of this work. A simple example that currently works quite well in most companies is sales. Once a corporation decides upon a revenue growth number, sales quotas are typically passed down through various geographic groupings to the individual salespeople. These salespeople are then measured against the established quotas. In a similar way, the ideal is to have *every* employee in the company have an equally direct alignment with the corporate goals. Individual performance metrics can provide this vehicle. These also provide us another opportunity to reinforce a systems way of working.

Reviewing the Strategy

Poor review of the strategy is another reason for its failure. Organizations start out with the best intentions, but sooner or later, operational priorities interfere with the attention that strategy requires.

As I have stated, movement of the organizational "whole" to a desired future state is a critical element of organizational success. Leaders need to understand and put in place an effective strategy execution process that successfully moves the members of the organization to this desired destination. Previously, we related statistics that highlight how poorly strategy execution is done in most companies. Engaging members of the organization in the strategy creation process is not enough; leaders must also "get them to the finish line."

The case, which I discussed in Chapter 2, turned out to be one of the best examples of strategic execution that I have ever seen. Because of its importance, I repeat a portion of it here. During the years when the Chairman had become less active, a new CEO had been chosen. I was involved with him and his direct reports in a strategic planning process. This process ended with a presentation to the CEO and his staff. I still remember clearly that when we talked about the execution of the plan, the CEO had stated very directly to his team that they would be reviewing the progress of the strategic plan at each of his staff meetings. It turns out they had indeed reviewed the progress of the plan at every staff meeting. They went on subsequently to have the best year in this company's 60-year history.

How we go about reviewing strategy is vitally dependent upon the culture of the company. We can also ask if the corporation as parent adds value to its parts, and contrariwise, if the parts add value to the whole. Both, as Russell Ackoff has stated, are necessary if we are to call the organization a system.

Inquiring further, we see that various degrees of planning influence and control influence are possible. These influences vary from very high involvement of the corporation in the planning activities of its business units, to a minimum involvement in planning with tight financial control. It would appear that no one approach is suitable for everyone. A company with a highly empowered, high trust culture might adopt a more hands-off approach, leaving the planning and control aspects largely to its business units and departments. On the other hand, a top-down, control-oriented culture would likely be heavily involved in the strategic planning and exercise tight controls as well.

Our discussion of the organization as system requires us to take a special view of control. As we will discuss later in detail in our section on corporate culture, a systemic way of working requires a culture that is empowering and trusting. This would suggest a more permissive, hands-off approach to control. In fact, as we shall see, strategy and culture provide us highly effective ways to maintain control in an organization.

Our present discussion is concerned with how we control the execution of the strategic plan. We have said that this involves measuring and reviewing its progress. A suitable question then is, "How and when should review of the strategic plan occur?" Also, what participation, if any, should the corporate office have in review of the functional plans?

Since individuals and functional groups have been involved in the development of the corporate strategy, and the plans of the functional groups have been built around the corporate goals, there is less of a need for the corporate office to review the latter's plans. Instead, the focus should be on the corporate office's review of the strategic plan of the enterprise. Questions at that level should basically ask:

- Are we meeting the milestones we have established?
- Why or why not?
- If we are not meeting the milestones, where should we begin to look for shortfalls?

Whichever style is adopted, I believe the review of strategy must be ongoing. One might, for example, conduct a *formal* review of strategy quarterly. This review could include members of the executive team and take place face-to-face. Planning units would review their departments prior to the corporate review.

Monthly, a less formal review might take place – either in writing or at the monthly staff meeting. The focus would continue to be on progress against performance metrics and exceptions to progress. Using the metrics described in the previous section, emphasis would be both on financial metrics and strategic metrics.

In the final analysis, we find no substitute, either in the change management literature, or in the area of strategy, for "what management pays attention to." There is no substitute for senior management asking almost on a daily basis, "How are we doing on the strategy? Why, or why isn't it, working? What issues stand in our way? What have we learned so far about the strategy? Does the strategy need to be changed?"

The review process also forms the basis for organizational learning. Part and parcel of the review process is learning what is working and what is not working and taking the necessary actions to correct the deficiencies. In reality, organizational learning should be part of every single step of the strategy process. As we create, communicate, validate and review the strategy, there should be a process in place that captures the learning and feeds the required actions back to update and revitalize the strategy.

Summary

In this chapter, we looked at the second major strategy process – namely, strategy execution. I discussed its historical failure, its causes, and proposed a model to enhance its chances of success. Once again, it is my hope that the strategic leader that I have described in this book will first strive to understand the model. Secondly, to use it as a vehicle to bring people, across functional divides, to work together for the greater good of the overall organization. And finally, at long last, to enjoy with them the desired destination they worked so hard to both create and attain!

References

1. Larry Bossidy & Ram Charan, *Execution: The Discipline of Getting Things Done* (Crown Business, 2002).
2. Greg Jaffe, "The Army Bets Its Battlefield Success on Soldiers Armed with Better Data," *Wall Street Journal*, March 30, 2001.

3. Michael Treacy & Fred Wiersema, *The Discipline of Market Leaders* (Addison-Wesley, 1995).
4. Peter S. DeLisi, "A Modern-Day Tragedy: The Digital Equipment Story," *Journal of Management Inquiry*, June 1998.
5. William D. Giles, "Making Strategy Work," *Long Range Planning*, October 1991.
6. Theodore Levitt, *The Marketing Imagination* (The Free Press, 1983).
7. Michel Robert, *Strategy Pure & Simple* (McGraw-Hill, 1993).
8. Robert S. Kaplan & David P. Norton, "The Balanced Scorecard – Measures That Drive Performance," *Harvard Business Review*, January–February 1992.
9. Robert S. Kaplan & David P. Norton, "Having Trouble with Your Strategy? Then Map It," *Harvard Business Review*, September–October 2000.

6 Organizational Culture

Introduction

The main theme of this book has dealt with the strategic leader and the impact of systems thinking on both the way we view organizations and the subsequent ways that the strategic leader influences them. I have argued that the strategic leader can most effectively influence the organization as system strategically and culturally. In the past two chapters, I have described how the strategy creation process and the strategy execution process can be used by the strategic leader to bring the people in the organization into an interdependent fabric focused on the overall good of the enterprise. Next, we will discuss corporate culture and its role in also enabling this occurrence.

In Chapter 2, "The New Strategic Leader," I highlighted the case study example of a client in the western U.S. that became my inspiration for the model that I have proposed in this book. The reader may remember that the Director of Strategic Planning and I had been asked to identify the strategic issues that stood in the way of the corporation's future success. This latter work identified a very large number of issues that we subsequently presented to the executive team. We also presented a very unanticipated solution to these issues – namely, a cultural solution. It turned out that resolving the issue of "What Kind of a Company Do You Want to Be?" addressed a majority of what were perceived to be strategic issues.

For me, this experience had a tremendous impact on me and taught me the fundamental importance of culture in my strategic work. As well, I witnessed the power of strategic processes, bringing people together across Divisions, to debate issues that faced the future of the company. Lastly, I saw great leadership that subsequently executed the plan that was developed and produced the best year in this company's 60-year history.

Corporate culture, when properly understood and employed, has the potential to unleash the creative talent and energy of the employees in the company. Some of this power derives from the sharing of values and core beliefs. When people share values and core beliefs, it unites them in a greater purpose. We speak, as it were, a "common language" with those people and become linked with them to preserve those beliefs. But despite this, there are certain cultures that do *not* foster the interdependence that I have argued is necessary for the organization to perform as a system.

Perhaps, it will be helpful before we begin an in-depth discussion about culture to give a few examples of the latter. Using case study examples throughout this chapter will be an effective way to transmit knowledge about culture – a subject that, in general, tends to be very poorly understood. From these examples, the reader will see that, like the human personality, culture has a pervasive influence on the individuals and the resulting performance of the organization.

A short but interesting example of a culture that did not foster interdependence is the large aerospace company that wanted to implement the then popular concept of "high performance teams." Like most aerospace companies, this company had throughout its history had much success with semi-permanent, formal, project teams. These teams were formed when a major defense program was won and continued through the life of the program. Examples might be a ballistic missile program, or a fighter aircraft program.

Unlike the program structure, however, the CEO of this enterprise had decided to extend the team concept further and put in place "high performance teams." In the latter concept, teams are a permanent way of working and are self-empowered. The team has the power to hire, fire and generally manage its own operation. As indicated earlier, project teams are semi-permanent. They are also empowered by management and do not run as if they were a separate business.

The other distinction that needs to be made is that certain teams are empowered by the assumptions of the culture. In other words, teaming is a natural way of doing things in this culture. An example that we will explore later is Digital Equipment Corporation (DEC). Its fundamental assumption or belief that "We are a family" led individuals naturally to team together. If a problem presented itself to a group of individuals, it was highly likely that these individuals would decide that they needed to form an informal group, i.e., a team, to address this problem. Unlike formal, project teams, this decision to act was *not* made by management. Once the problem was solved, or went away, the informal team at DEC disbanded itself.

My main exposure to this aerospace client was a senior management meeting attended by 45 of its senior executives. The purpose of the meeting was to educate and to focus the management on the concept of "high performance teams." My role was to observe the meeting and to subsequently report my findings to the CEO.

Prior to the meeting, I had done some consulting work with another group within the company. This work had given me the opportunity to begin to observe the unique culture of this organization. What I had learned was that the culture had been heavily influenced by its legendary founder. In its truest sense, this individual was a western type hero and had made a mark in many diverse fields. Not surprisingly, this identification with its founder had produced a rugged, individualistic culture within the company.

The previous observations about the culture, plus the meeting that I attended, gave me an excellent opportunity to draw some conclusions about the organization's chances to implement "high performance teams." I don't recall many specifics from the meeting; I only recall that individuals acted at the meeting consistent with my earlier observations about the culture. These were clearly individuals "acting on their own stage" and being singled out for individual performance – not group activity.

I later reported to the CEO that, in my estimation, their chances of implementing "high performance teams" were very poor. To support my argument, I proceeded to relate my understanding of their culture and its influence from its founder. My recommendation was that they stick with the successful project teams that were part of their history.

Since my role with this client was a secondary one, I subsequently lost direct contact with the management team. Some months later, I learned that they had indeed tried to implement the "high performance team" concept, but that it had failed. Fortunately in this case, the fate of the company was not at stake, as we see in some cases where the strategy is directly affected. For us, this case uniquely illustrates the dependence of even organizational structure and ways of working on the culture of the company.

The Company That Had No Heroes

It might also be obvious that interdependence cannot exist unless the parties trust one another. The next case illustrates this and it is also significant because it highlights some of the other tools that can be used in cultural work. Lastly, this case also is an example of the classic consulting problem that the main issue we are often brought in to address is not always the real problem. In the case I am about to relate, the presenting symptom was significant conflict between the departments of a small defense contractor.

Over the years, my approach to conflict resolution and team building has changed significantly. In the earlier years, I was inclined to use a variety of techniques to surface the conflict and to deal constructively with it. As a strategy consultant, I learned, however, that many times team building just seemed to happen as a byproduct of getting groups together to develop a galvanizing vision for the organization. *(The reader will note that in an earlier chapter, I indicated that consulting examples led me to my theory that I could use the strategy processes to enable organizational interdependence.)* I decided, therefore, to use this latter approach with the defense contractor.

As before, I used a workshop approach in which I brought the participants together for a very intensive two days. Starting with a form of strategic planning, I felt good about the progress and was optimistic that the conflict resolution I sought would somehow eventually become a byproduct of the session. About halfway through the session, however, the visible conflict and animosity between the groups could no longer be ignored. I decided to try a cultural approach to see if I could somehow bring the groups together at the level of shared values. What happened, however, was a surprise even to me.

One of the tools I have borrowed from Ed Schein involves inquiries about the heroes of the culture. The idea is simple – identifying heroes, what they stood for, and why they are considered heroes, sometimes gives us a clue about attributes of the culture. Heroes can be the ultimate embodiment of the culture.

After some preliminary cultural discussions with the group, I asked them to identify people that they would consider cultural heroes. A period of silence ensued, after which I repeated the question, "Tell me about some of your cultural heroes." Once again, silence followed. One individual finally said to me, "We have no heroes." Incredulous, I asserted that I had never experienced a culture that didn't have at least one hero. "Surely, you must have one," but again, the response came back, "We have no heroes."

Not wanting to give up, I turned my attention to people who were considered to be company outcasts or "villains." One individual was identified and described to me. I was to learn a valuable lesson from this – in some repressive cultures, certain people stand out because they fought the culture and survived. These people can be considered counter-cultural heroes and we can learn a lot about the company culture by studying what they fought for and resented in the parent culture.

To bring this case to a conclusion, I need to mention the outcome of my search for cultural heroes. After conceding that maybe this culture really had no heroes, and as part of another exercise, I asked the group to identify for me the type of individual they hire. Once again, the theory is that companies hire people that will fit into the culture. Investigating, therefore, the qualities of the people that they hire, should tell us something about the culture.

My questioning went like this: "Would you hire someone that stands out as an individual, as opposed to a team player?" The answer was, "No." "Would you hire someone that was very bright – yet, somewhat of a maverick?" Again, the answer was, "No." "Would you hire a risk-taker?" "No," was the reply. Additional questions supported the profile of a passive individual that "didn't make any waves." Finally, someone in the audience commented, "Pete, do you see why we don't have any heroes?"

Generally, I make it quite clear to my clients that culture is not good or bad, right or wrong; rather, it either is an enabler to their strategy, or an inhibitor. Because of the difficulty of cultural change when the culture is an inhibitor to the strategy, I usually recommend to the client that they change the strategy. In the above instance, we truly had the rare case of a dysfunctional culture. My recommendation was to change the culture.

Cultural Basics

Earlier, we discussed New Age thinking and the role that it played in contemporary organizations. We said that it provided organizations a collaborative, empowered way of working, and an effective method to deal with the dynamic, changing times. But as I have argued, what these ways of thinking by themselves lack is the shared destination that is participatively developed in the strategy creation process. They also lack an effective process of strategy execution, which engages them and moves them as a "whole" to a realization of that chosen destination. In other words, there are ways we can get individuals and groups to work together collaboratively, and even interdependently. While I argued in Chapter 3 that this may be a standalone good for the organization, if their efforts are not means to a clear set of performance goals, the efforts will be suboptimal.

Let us turn then to a more detailed discussion of corporate culture and its role. For our purposes, we might consider corporate culture as part of New Age thinking. As I indicated earlier, its first serious appearance was in the early 1980s, and it has since played a prominent role in corporate life. Unlike many of the other New Age models that have come and gone, corporate culture has drawn many respected followers and continues to grow. For this reason, and for its ability to enable the desired results I have outlined, I have chosen it as a major element of the proposed model in this book.

We will view corporate culture as one element of the total solution that I have proposed. As the reader may recall, this includes systems thinking and the processes of strategy creation and strategy execution. Culture's role is to provide a climate that unleashes the creative talent and energy of the people as they participate in both the creation and execution of the organization's overall strategy.

My emphasis in this chapter will be on developing a solid, working understanding of corporate culture. As part of this, I will introduce several models that will help us both understand culture and apply it to one's corporation. Other sections will address further elaboration of culture's role in the organization as system and its role in the strategic operational model that we previously introduced. Case studies from my own consulting experiences will further clarify our content.

For much of the content of this chapter, I am deeply indebted to Dr. Edgar Schein, professor emeritus at the MIT Sloan school, who has been my mentor for the past 30 years and has taught me so very much about the subject of organizational culture. I will begin with his definition of culture.

> A pattern of shared basic assumptions that the group learned as it solved its problems of external adaptation and internal integration, that has worked well enough to be considered valid and, therefore, to be taught to new members as the correct way to perceive, think, and feel in relation to those problems.[1]

From the definition, we see that culture is a pattern. It is important to keep this in mind as we discuss other aspects of culture. Secondly, it is a pattern of shared basic assumptions. We will look at some examples of this, but essentially, these are deeply rooted core beliefs. The group learned these basic assumptions through solving problems that existed on the outside of the corporation. This might be, for example, competing in a new marketplace. The group also learned the basic assumptions through internal integration. An example might be getting groups to work together effectively across functional boundaries. As a result of solving these problems, the culture is considered valid and is therefore taught to new members as the correct way to deal with similar problems.

A useful model for understanding and dealing with culture is the lily pond analogy, shown in Figure 6.1. It is an effective way to view the various levels that comprise the system of culture. Its origin, I believe, dates back to work done by a colleague of mine at Digital Equipment Corporation, John Scorzoni.

In the development of the analogy, we start on the surface of the lily pond. There we see an individual lily pad with its leaves and flowers lying on the surface of the water. Beneath the surface, we see a supporting stem, eventually rooted in nurturing mire and muck at the bottom of the water.

In an analogous way, on the surface of culture we see its visible components – items such as behaviors, artifacts and stories that are told. Digging beneath the surface, we see the values that are important to the organization and held dearly by them. These values are conscious and are debatable, but as Ed Schein maintains, over time if they work in solving the problems of external adaptation and internal integration, they are taken for granted and become deeply rooted. They now become the unconscious assumptions of the culture. The analogy helps us to understand the difficulty of dealing with culture. Because the assumptions are unconscious and deeply rooted, they are very difficult to both discern and change.

It might be useful at this point to show an example of how the lily pond analogy would work in an actual case. For this, I will again draw upon my former employer, Digital Equipment Corporation.

In the case of Digital, there were certain behaviors that were visible on the surface. These included the way new employees were hired, assignment of perks, such as parking spots and offices, how decisions were made, how people moved from one job to another, and how people were terminated. The surface behaviors, however, would not tell us much about the culture. For this, we would need to drill down to the levels of values and basic assumptions. These latter items surfaced in research that I did while working at the company.

At the values level, we see three strong values that supported the surface behaviors that we have mentioned. These were career employment,

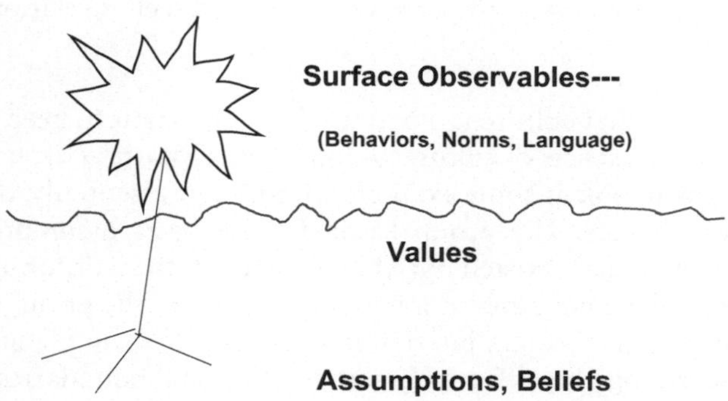

Figure 6.1 Lily Pond Analogy.

egalitarianism and team play/consensus decision-making. Interviews of new employees tended to be endless at Digital. Although I had been aggressively recruited, it felt strangely like the courtship process in my parents' native Sicily. Everyone got to say whether they liked me or not – my prospective boss, his boss, his boss's boss, prospective peers, prospective subordinates, administrative support people and a few others thrown in for good measure. Egalitarianism was obvious from the lack of special parking spots and fancy offices for senior executives. Senior executives had cubicles just like the rest of the employees.

In addition to the extensive interviews which I had experienced earlier, I was to learn about teamplay/consensus decision-making, and "buy-in." At first it appeared incongruous to me; people would fight vigorously over ideas, and yet really seemed to care about teamwork. It wasn't just words. Teams existed at every level. I also got my first lesson in the "veto power" of the Digital culture. Whereas it was true that the people in Digital were tremendously empowered, it was also true that they had to get the "buy-in" of all those affected by their proposed actions. This could lead to endless rounds of meetings, negotiations and frustration. I was later to describe this phenomenon by complaining that, "It seems that everyone in Digital can say 'no,' but no one can say 'yes.' "

Later in my career, I was to learn the reason behind the extensive interview process – newcomers weren't just joining another company; they were joining the "Digital family," and therefore had to be approved by the other significant members of this family. This core belief filled in for me the rest of the pattern. The reason that there were no special perks, people weren't laid off, and others had to buy in to your decisions, was that "Digital was a family." This was one of the fundamental assumptions of the culture as we see now in Figure 6.2.

Later, I was to experience the individual autonomy and empowerment that existed in the Digital culture. Once again, I was to contrast this with my previous IBM experience by making the observation that it seemed to me like a

Figure 6.2 Assumption About Relationships.

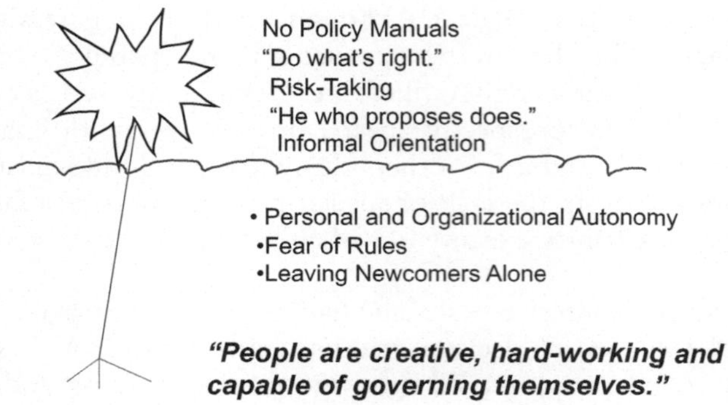

Figure 6.3 Assumption About People.

"good news/bad news" type story. The good news about IBM was that whatever responsibility you were given, you owned the whole thing. The bad news was that it was extremely small. The good news about Digital was that you could assume whatever responsibility you wished. The bad news was – so could everyone else. And as a result, many people ended up doing the same things.

I was to learn that it didn't make any difference where you were in the organization. If you saw an opportunity and you believed you had the talent to apply to it, you could make a proposal and be assigned the responsibility to carry it out. "He who proposes does," was more than an accepted practice; it was a deeply held value of the company.

Figure 6.3 is another exhibit showing the lily pond and Digital's basic assumption about people.

We see here once again the surface observables and the underlying values eventually lead us to the basic assumption that, "People are creative, hard-working and capable of governing themselves." There were other basic assumptions that made up the Digital culture, but since we are using Digital in the lily pond analogy only to highlight a model for understanding culture, we will not go into these other assumptions.

Having basically defined culture, and having introduced the lily pond analogy, let us turn our attention to the role that organizational culture plays in the organization as system. Previously, I mentioned that there are certain cultural attributes that are necessary to enable the organization to function as a system. I have identified these attributes as collaboration, participation and empowerment. Going further, it would be highly desirable for these attributes to lead optimally to a state of interdependence, the state that is truly the "sine qua non" of a system.

Referring to the cultural grid in Figures 6.4 and 6.5, we could argue that it is the "entrepreneurialism" culture that would most closely enable interdependence. The "professional management" culture, with its emphasis on control and authority, would not seem to produce the same result. An example from my

Entrepreneurial	Professional Management
Empowerment	Control
Internal Controls	External Controls
Shared Authority	Authority at the Top
Shared Responsibility	Accountability
Ownership	"Pass the Buck"
Network, Teams, Matrix	Hierarchy, SBU
Decentralized	Centralized
Innovation	Standardization
Customize	Mass Produce
Intuition	Scientific Mgt.
Risk-Taking	Conservative

Figure 6.4 Cultural Dilemmas.

Entrepreneurial	Professional Management
High Trust	Suspicion
Truth Through Conflict	Conflict Avoidant
Consensus Decisions	Authority Decisions
"Buy-In"	Individual Latitude
Frequent Meetings	"Power" Meets
Inefficiency	Efficiency
Potential Chaos	Disciplined
High Comm. Bandwidth	Narrow Bandwidth
Organizational Learning	Narrowness
Cross-Functional	"Stovepipes"
Collaborative	Individualistic

Figure 6.5 Cultural Dilemmas.

consulting experience might highlight this latter condition. This example will also remind us that the model that I have proposed in this book is about enhancing organizational performance, and that cultures that enable performance-enabling attributes, such as innovation, would be highly desirable.

The "Whack a Mole" Culture

Some years ago, I was approached by a division of a major oil company. They explained to me that they weren't sure, but they thought that their culture was a serious inhibitor to their success. "Was there anything I could do to help?" they asked.

This was the research division of the oil company. It was staffed by very bright, educated scientists – many of them with Ph.D. degrees. As with many research groups, their mission dealt with bringing innovative, new products to market faster than their competition. This was not happening, and for some reason, they felt that culture had something to do with it.

After some preliminary work with members of the staff, I proceeded to conduct a half-day workshop with key members of the division. In this workshop,

I used a number of techniques and tools to get a better understanding of the cultural dynamics. The lily pond analogy was one of these tools.

Using the lily pond, we started by examining the surface aspects of the culture. I inquired about the behaviors and artifacts that were visible to them and we listed them. As with most cultural inquiries, one never knows what it is that will provide a significant clue to the underlying cultural dynamics. In this case, we spent some time on the surface aspects without much resulting significance.

The break came when I asked if there were any stories that they knew to have circulated around the company and were told repeatedly over the years. One participant related a story which was to subsequently capture the essence of this culture. He mentioned that one of the corporate vice presidents had once done a presentation to a group of people within the company. Embedded in the presentation were some financial figures. During the presentation, as the vice president was describing these numbers, one of the junior individuals in the audience raised his hand and proceeded to point out to the vice president that one of the financial totals was wrong. Agreeing with the observation, the vice president thanked him and continued with the presentation.

After the presentation was completed, the supervisor of the individual that had pointed out the financial error approached him and proceeded to chastise him for correcting a vice president of the company in public. "Don't you ever correct an executive of this company in this manner again," was his parting comment as he left. This story had survived over the years, was told repeatedly, and had now become representative of "how we do things around here."

We next proceeded to get below the surface of the lily pond and to discuss the values of the organization. After much discussion, the group homed in on another piece of the cultural puzzle. They went on to describe their three primary values as being: *risk-averse, reactive and conflict-avoidant.* Already, all of us were beginning to see that these were not exactly the values that one typically associates with organizations that are highly dependent on creativity for their success.

The last part of the workshop dealt with the fundamental assumptions of the culture. As so often happens, the exact wording of the assumptions does not surface until sometime later, but the pattern of the culture was starting to become clear. It was captured dramatically by one of the participants near the end of the workshop. In cultural workshops of this type, I will often try to bring things together in some way. I'll use a variety of techniques to accomplish the synthesis and integration that is necessary at this point.

One of these techniques is to walk over to a flipchart and ask the participants to complete the following statement: "We're like …" A variety of free-flowing responses usually result, but not always with the magic of this particular occasion. After a number of random responses, one of the scientists raised his hand and proceeded to say, "We're like a giant in manacles." As he said this, a hush came over the room and we sensed that he "had just broken the code." I asked him to clarify what he meant, and he responded, "Here we are all these very bright scientists, but our hands are tied by the culture. Every time we raise our heads up, we are knocked down."

Immediately, the image of the kids' arcade game, whack a mole, jumped into my head. In this game, children are given a small mallet with which to smash down tiny little creatures as they surface randomly and rapidly from a number of circular openings. Similar to the game, individuals in this culture dared not raise their head for fear of being struck down.

So often I have learned that certain cultures contain within themselves the very things that maintain their inertia and prevent them from changing. In this particular case, we laid out an action plan that would have started the division on a path to more favorably align the culture with the mission of the organization. Sadly, as I feared, the plan never saw the light of day. Fear of "raising their heads" made it all but impossible for them to bring the matter to the attention of senior management.

In the case I have just described, we see the example of an organization whose culture inhibited the accomplishment of its main mission – namely, bringing innovative, new products to market. Its culture would not enable the participative, empowered kind of working that would have made this possible. We see here also a good example of the powerful role that culture plays in our model of the systemic organization.

The next example is of a company that had a participative, empowered culture. Its culture on the grid that we described earlier was strongly "entrepreneurial." The company enjoyed success for many years and was later acquired by a company that had a very strong "professional management" culture. What can we learn from the merger of these two diverse cultures? And what lessons does it teach us about culture in general?

"Freedom Is Good, but Control Is Better"

The above quote is attributed to Vladimir Lenin. It's a fitting theme for our next case and highlights the difficulty of continued growth, the perils of mergers and acquisitions and the role that culture plays in both. While this case does not appear to bear directly upon culture's role in the systemic organization, I believe it broadens the reader's understanding of culture, and therefore supports my argument that certain chapters of my book can be standalone sources of important organizational knowledge.

Toward the end of the 90s, I consulted with a small ($100 million) enterprise. This was a typical, high-tech, Silicon Valley startup. We will call this company NEWCO. Growth was very rapid for this firm; they were able to double their revenues every year. Unlike many startups, they also realized before they got into trouble that they needed to bring in senior managers to run the business. They did this and brought in a talented team of senior executives with extensive industry experience.

Everything seemed to be going in the right direction for NEWCO, as they set their sights on $1 billion of revenue over the ensuing years. It was somewhat of a surprise, therefore, when it was announced that they were going to be bought, for a very generous sum, by the largest company in their industry. The latter company (one that we will refer to as OLDCO), a $20 billion enterprise, realized that for them to continue growing, they needed to enter new industry segments. Rather than developing the required expertise on their own, they decided to buy a company that was already very successful in this new, emerging market – seemingly a very wise move.

At the time of the acquisition, the parent company displayed further wisdom by announcing that their plans were to leave the small company alone and to let them maintain their separate identity. "After all," it was announced, "you have been very successful without us." Within the next 12 months, this promise was to be severely broken.

During the transition to the new company, I was asked to stay on by NEWCO and to lend whatever assistance I could – especially with the cultural integration of the two organizations. I don't remember exactly when it happened, but I do remember the event that signified that the promise was about to be broken.

One day, it was announced suddenly that over the next weekend, individuals from the parent company would be coming in to replace all the signs that displayed NEWCO's name. In their place, the name of the acquiring company would be prominently displayed. In the weeks and months that followed, the appearance of OLDCO's management in the day-by-day running of the business also became much more visible and newer, more formal processes were imposed on the acquired company. It was apparent that "the honeymoon was over."

By the end of that first year after the acquisition, little remained of NEWCO's identity. People began to leave and to take with them the intellectual capital that the parent company had paid $2.3 billion for. It was obvious that another statistic was about to be added to the long list of failed acquisitions.

Let us look now at the cultural issues that led to the failure of this acquisition and see what we can learn from them. We will use Figures 6.4 and 6.5 for this purpose. Over the years, I have continued to enhance this tool and found it to be one of the most powerful cultural tools that I have in working with client companies.

As we look at the cultural grids, we see several things. First of all, we see the pattern of culture that Ed Schein describes very clearly. When we focus on the pattern, we know almost intuitively that the attributes of the entrepreneurial culture hang together quite nicely and are different from the attributes of the professional management culture. A second thing that one might observe is that the transition from one culture to the other is a matter of degrees. In other words, we can view the exhibit as a continuum, rather than viewing its contents as absolute entities. It becomes possible, then, for us to put almost any organizational culture on this continuum by identifying the degree of each attribute that it contains. A word of caution, however, this is not an exact science and should not be used as the sole means of inquiry. It is one of many tools that should be used in gaining a picture of an organization's cultural pattern.

If we return to our discussion of the NEWCO case, we see that NEWCO had an entrepreneurial culture, whereas OLDCO had a strong professional management culture. To compete in the newly emerging market space that the parent company had targeted, the entrepreneurial culture was a definite asset. Qualities such as innovation, risk-taking and rapid time to market were essential in this dynamic, competitive marketplace. On the other hand, the professional management culture was very appropriate for the parent company, whose growth was in a low margin, commodity business, driven by cost concerns. Very significantly, at one time, early in its history, the parent company had an entrepreneurial culture. In fact, it is one of the only companies that I have ever seen that has *successfully* made the transition from the entrepreneurial side to the professional management side when its markets matured and it needed to.

It appears now that what happened was that OLDCO succumbed to the temptations of the control-oriented, professional management culture. Not unlike the obsessive-compulsive personality in the field of psychology, OLDCO couldn't let go. Processes and controls became ends in themselves, rather than being viewed as means to a greater end.

Interestingly, attempts were made to deal with the cultural conflict. In a series of sessions over a period of months with both management teams, I used Figures 6.4 and 6.5 to highlight the problems in culturally integrating the two companies. We even assigned numbers for each attribute to indicate where they currently were and where they wanted to be. They recognized that they needed to move to the entrepreneurial side, but couldn't give up the controls, efficiencies and accountability of the professional management culture. The effort languished and finally died. The parent company eventually ended up writing off the $2.3 billion they had spent on the acquisition.

What could OLDCO have done? It is perhaps obvious to the reader that they should have left NEWCO alone to run their own business, with their own culture. We have successful examples of this in industry. Lockheed and their SR 71 skunk works comes to mind, as well as IBM and its birth of the PC. Both of these companies had strong professional management cultures at the time – yet, were able to let go and achieved significant success in the process. Maybe, the answer is that movement too far in either the entrepreneurial or professional management direction can be disastrous. OLDCO clearly had moved too far on the professional management side.

In the last two examples that I have described, we see failures of culture. In both cases, we see strong, dominant, parent cultures that valued "professional management" over the "entrepreneurial" type culture. We have argued that the latter culture enables the system kind of working that is beneficial for enhanced corporate performance.

The reader might be curious to know what has happened to the two parent companies that I have described. Both of them have retained their "professional management" cultures. As we mentioned, in the case of OLDCO versus NEWCO, the parent company ended up writing off the $2.3 billion investment they had made in the acquired company, but the company continues to be successful overall. In the case of the oil company, the parent company also continues to be successful.

The success of these two companies does not negate the value of the model that I have proposed in this book. As I maintained very early in my introduction, there are many ways for companies to be successful. Both of these examples were very large companies that had been successful prior to my involvement with them. I have previously indicated that the "professional management" culture is beneficial to large organizations that compete on a cost basis, and therefore, desire controls, accountability and efficiencies. While the systemic model that I have proposed in this book may not be either desirable or attainable for these two companies, there is no reason to believe that these companies will not continue to be successful in the future. It also begs the question, "What kind of company is best suited for the systemic model?"

Positioning the Systemic Model

In this book, I have argued for a highly integrated model that includes the following characteristics:

- An organization exhibiting systemic interdependence between parts of the organization.
- Strategy processes that enable effective interactions between functions and that focus the results of those interactions on the "whole." I have suggested that the "whole" is best represented by a shared set of corporate goals.
- A corporate culture that is collaborative, participative and empowered. I have suggested that the "entrepreneurial" culture depicted on our culture grid is an example.

From our discussion that we have just concluded, we see that one of the major limiting factors in getting an organization to become systemic is the culture of the organization. A "professional management" culture does not provide the fabric that enables effective participation and interaction. But we have also just seen that these kinds of companies can nonetheless be successful. What do we conclude then?

Is it possible to change an organization's culture? Or minimally, is it possible to change those aspects of culture that focus on participation and empowerment? I believe the latter is possible and was encouraged by the following example from my consulting work.

A Learning Culture

A few years ago, I was asked by a Silicon Valley company to help them develop a sales strategy for the company. Over the ensuing months, a number of activities produced a picture of where this company was and where it wanted to go. Emerging from this process was the recognition that products and technologies were no longer an instant formula for success. Competitive differentiation for this company was harder and harder to achieve through products alone. It was decided to pursue a strategy that had been written about for years, but poorly executed in most cases. The company decided to pursue a strategy based upon "knowledge." A more specific rendering of this strategy was, "Sustainable differentiation is based upon learning faster than your competition."

I have already indicated how central culture has been in each and every one of my strategy engagements. Accordingly, we then proceeded to investigate whether the existing culture would enable the desired strategy. What we found was a culture that was closed – one in which information would not flow freely between elements of the enterprise and its environment. For example, the company would not willingly share certain information with customers, because of the fear that it would get in the hands of competition. As well, the field would not share information with headquarters, and headquarters with the field. Departments would also not share information with other departments.

Underlying this culture was a history of leadership at the hands of an autocratic, top-down, control-oriented CEO. We would characterize them as being at the professional management side of Figures 6.4 and 6.5. This focus, as I have described in some previous cases, had produced an operationally excellent company, with solid efficiencies and resulting high margins. It paid a price, however, in the morale and empowerment of its people.

The "knowledge" strategy was introduced after the retirement of the former CEO and was actively supported by the new CEO. But, as previously mentioned, the existing culture did not support the new strategy. At this point, we had to decide whether to change the strategy, or to change the culture. With the arrival of a new CEO enhancing our chances of success, I recommended that they change the culture. More significantly, the new CEO had already communicated his desire to change the existing culture. The question now became, "What should we change the culture to?"

A powerful lesson had just emerged for me in the process – namely, that if we can be very clear about the strategic behaviors that we want, then we can focus the culture change on much smaller elements. In my experience, culture change efforts that focus on changing the overall culture are doomed to failure. As we will see, our chances of success are enhanced by limiting the culture change to only those elements that are truly needed to enable the desired strategic behaviors.

In our case, we knew that data and information would have to flow quickly from a variety of "touch points" with customers and the environment. In turn, these would have to be converted effectively into patterns of knowledge about customers, the marketplace and competition. It was obvious to us that a culture in which no one trusted anyone with the required information would never enable the desired strategy.

To begin the process of cultural change, I laid out a set of values that I thought would encourage our further dialogue. Once again, it is important to highlight the role of values in this process. While the true essence of culture is determined at the level of fundamental assumptions, it is values that give us the opportunity to consciously debate cultural issues.

After some active discussion, following is the list of values that emerged and represented the shift from the existing culture to the desired culture:

- Empowering
- Trusting
- Teaming
- Fast-Moving
- Reasonably Risk-Taking
- Customer-Centered
- Innovative
- A Learning Culture

It is hopefully obvious how the above listed values would produce behaviors that enable the knowledge strategy that I have described. In this culture, people would trust one another with information and it would flow quickly between individuals and groups. Being close to the customer would enhance the value of the information, and a focus on learning would lead people to constantly ask about the ultimate implications and pattern of the information.

Two years after the culture change strategy that I have just described went into place, I had the opportunity to go back and do some further work with the client. To my pleasant surprise, the client's culture had indeed changed in the desired direction. Work still remains to be done, but already the client is focusing their efforts and mine on a refinement of the knowledge strategy. The culture is no longer an inhibitor and a greater degree of trust exists at all levels of the enterprise. For example, whereas before a customer would not be told about certain product problems until the problem had been resolved, now customers complimented the company on their "openness" about such problems. More significantly, the knowledge strategy is producing competitive results. Market share gains against their primary competitor are clearly visible.

The lessons from this last case are noteworthy. Its short-term success has restored my confidence in culture change in general. To summarize the lessons, it has taught me that, "You can't change *the* culture; you can only change portions of the culture." This, in turn, leads us to be clear about what specific strategic behaviors we need to change and why. Our further discussion leads us to a focus on the values that would support these behaviors. Embedding new fundamental assumptions would appear to be the final conclusive step, but I am encouraged that, in this case, we really didn't do this. A focus on the desired behavioral and value changes, plus the arrival of the new CEO and other senior managers from outside, seem to have made the changes possible. Time will tell how permanent and successful these will be.

Before leaving this chapter, there is one other major issue that we should address. The reader will probably have noted that I have strongly asserted that the attributes of the "entrepreneurial" type culture are necessary in order for people to be able to work effectively as members of the organization as system. In other words, I am saying that the model that I have proposed in this book would not work, for example, in a company with a "professional management" culture. Later, in the chapter on "Getting Started," I will deal specifically with this question, but for now, let me say that the "Learning Culture" case that I just presented has given me some confidence that the benefits of the model I have proposed in this book are possible even for the top-down, "professional management" culture.

Reference

1. Edgar H. Schein, *Organizational Culture and Leadership*, Third Edition (Jossey-Bass, 2004).

7 Leadership of the Organization as System

Introduction

In Chapter 2, I introduced the main theme of the book and we looked at the influence of systems thinking on strategic leadership. I also provided an overview of a series of leadership actions that were necessary to enable the resulting systems way of working. Later, I indicated, I would treat the subject of this unique form of leadership in greater detail.

A large number of books have been written about the subject of leadership. It is as if the answer to many of our industrial problems is, "leadership;" sadly, we don't always know what the question is. In this chapter, I would like to take a unique look at leadership. By focusing on leadership of the organization as system, I believe I avoid overlap with many of the books that have been written about the generic qualities of leadership. In the second part of this chapter, however, I will stray somewhat from this promise.

In substantial portions of this book, I have dealt with a primary skill of leadership – namely, the skill of influence. In the case of the strategic leader, I have argued that he uniquely influences the organizational system, and moves it to a desired future state, strategically and culturally. But what of interpersonal influence? Is that not important? Do I not have anything unique to say about this? In a later portion of this chapter, I will draw upon my extensive experience in sales, marketing and consulting, to write about interpersonal influence. Also, where possible, I will tailor my comments for an audience that is often ignored in the leadership literature – those individuals below the top.

Let us turn now to a discussion of the type of leadership that is necessary in the organization as system. We could start, for example, and ask if the leaders of interdependent organizations need to have different skills. I would argue that the ability to combine themes and ideas from different disciplines and functions in new insightful ways will require the future manager to become much more of a "general manager." She will continue to have an in-depth specialty; however, she will need to understand much better the interrelationships of her function and discipline with the others in the organization.

Symbolically, I like the "T" concept originally coined by Marco Iansiti, from the Harvard Business School.[1] The vertical portion of the "T" corresponds to the in-depth specialty, while the horizontal line corresponds to the linkages and interdependencies between the subject specialty and the other specialties in the organization. We have all worked on the vertical portion of this T; we now need to figure out how to work better on the horizontal portion.

In the introduction to the book, I suggested that this book is about a new leadership for our times. As I have discussed, it is leadership of an organizational system and the interactions of that system. I have also argued that there are only two ways to effectively lead the organizational system – strategically and culturally. In this chapter, I will summarize some of our discussion, expand upon it as necessary, and offer specific tips that leaders can use to derive maximum benefit from the organizational system.

In this chapter, I will expand upon the leadership actions that I originally included in the chapter on "The New Strategic Leader." To give examples of their practical use, I will also add relevant cases from my consulting experience.

Maximizing the Effectiveness of the "New Strategic Leader"

In Order to Lead the Organization as System, Strategic Leaders Should Do the Following:

1. Leaders of the organizational system should get its members to focus on the "whole." This "whole" is the overall good of the enterprise. As I have further defined, this is best represented by the long-term goals that members of the organization have helped to create and which define success for the organization. We know from change theory that "what leaders pay attention to," is an effective way to get members of the organization to do the same; therefore, leaders should call constant attention to the "whole."

One way that leaders can make the "whole" visible to the members of the organization is by showing them the interrelationships that can make the company stronger and more successful. For me, the best example of this has been the founder of the company in the western U.S. that I referenced in my case example in Chapter 2. Earlier I mentioned how he somehow saw his businesses all interrelated.

2. An additional element of the model that I have proposed in this book is the interdependent workings of the members of the organization and the vertical integration of their results into the "whole." Strategic leaders need to understand how to accomplish this. I believe that my chapters on strategy and culture outline the necessary steps. The "silos" from the Newton/Descartes era continue to exist. As W. Robinson stated in his 1925 *Harvard Business Review* article,[2] unless leaders take specific actions to bridge the gaps between functions, the natural functional bias to separate them will prevail.

I have shown how the strategy processes, and especially clear strategic choices, can help create interdependence between groups. Also, in Chapter 3, using a systemic operational model, I have introduced a number of other ways, for example, the use of business processes, management systems and information technology, to create interdependence.

3. Borrowing from Russell Ackoff, strategic leaders need to manage the interactions between the parts of the system. What does this mean and how does the leader accomplish this? Like getting others to pay attention to the "whole," the strategic leader manages system interactions by calling attention to them. A good example of this is the client knowledge system that I discussed earlier. In the proposed program, the intent was to have members of the corporation share their customer knowledge with others in the organization. I related that this effort was unsuccessful, because of the culture of the organization. An effective strategic leader, faced with the same situation, might manage the interactions between different departments by first making the whole organization aware of the importance of getting everyone's knowledge into the customer knowledge system. Next, he would ask each department that he encountered, "Where do we stand on getting your knowledge of our customers together with the knowledge from our other departments?"
4. Leaders of the organizational system must become knowledgeable about strategy processes. In addition, they should take steps to embed this knowledge appropriately into their organization. Leaders do not come up through a strategy function, and there are few other good ways to learn strategy; therefore, special steps need to be taken in order to acquire the requisite knowledge. *Potential competitive advantage from this move makes this a very worthwhile activity.*

Given the importance I am ascribing to strategy, what then can senior executives do in order to develop a greater understanding of strategy and its components? While this might be a subject for a whole separate discussion, following are a few brief suggestions.

- Educate yourself and the executive team. Look for a program that will teach you the elements of strategy that I have outlined and that has a practical orientation. Short workshops for the executive team, conducted by an outside resource, could also be an option.
- Read good strategic material. The *Harvard Business Review* and *Sloan Management Review* are excellent sources. In addition, a number of the large strategy consulting firms offer newsletters that contain a wealth of practical knowledge. Circulate good articles to the rest of the executive team and use them, for example, as a forum for discussion at executive staff meetings.

- Use outsiders selectively. There are advantages to using outside strategy consultants. In addition to helping with the strategy process, they can be a further source of knowledge for the executive team.
- Think about creating a strategy function within the corporation. Alternatively, hire a strong strategy person. Again, this person can be invaluable in helping the corporation develop a future direction, and can also serve to stimulate strategic thinking within the corporation.
- Spend time talking about strategy with the senior executive team. Research that I did some years ago revealed that 85 percent of executive teams spend less than an hour a month on strategy. Perhaps this has improved since, but my experience suggests it still could be a lot better. One of the most successful strategy engagements that I have had was with a corporation whose CEO said that they would review progress on their strategic plan at every senior staff meeting. This company went on to have its most successful year in its very long history.

Earlier, I mentioned developing the structural concept, The General Manager of Strategic Resources. This organizational subsystem included HR, IT and a strategy function. I lean toward having companies appoint someone as head of strategy for the company. Whether it be as part of the general manager role, or separately, it still is a major opportunity for most companies. Over the years, some companies have appointed a Chief Strategy Officer (CSO). As I write this, it once again appears to be in vogue.

How would one find a good CSO? I believe the CIO would be a good candidate. In fact, a number of corporations have already appointed their CIO as CSO. Although CIOs have not enjoyed great reputations in many companies, there are some very talented ones around. A CIO tends to have a systemic view of the organization. Their work involves looking across the whole organization and seeing how parts of the company are connected with the whole. When developing an application for a department, for example, they look at how the application will affect other departments in the company. For years, they truly have worked as a systems-oriented organization.

Whether or not the CIO would be a good CSO candidate, the company should look for someone who is a good general manager and can look across the organization. He or she may not have much strategy knowledge, but this can be acquired. This individual can be effective and valuable in a number of ways. In addition to leading the strategic, annual, planning process, this individual can work on mergers and acquisitions and the strategy execution process. The latter can be a full-time job for many individuals. The strategy creation process can also require a great amount of work. Strategy is no longer a document that gets developed and rests on the shelf for the duration of its life; it should be a continuous process. Therefore, a CSO should constantly monitor trends, competition and other things that might disrupt the company's strategy.

5. Strategic leaders must also become knowledgeable about organizational culture. There is tremendous confusion about culture, what it is, and its implications for the organization. Some leaders have tended to dismiss it as a soft skill the Human Resources organization should worry about. In this book, I have provided the leader some practical cultural basics that they can use with their leadership teams. As I have tried to do, I have stressed the role of culture as an enabler to organizational success – not as a standalone entity. Leadership teams can use the material from this book to investigate this dynamic in their organization.

The cultural stories that I have highlighted have hopefully conveyed the importance of organizational culture. A number of stories have shown the role of culture in the failure of mergers and in other situations. Other stories have also illustrated that, unlike strategy, leaders do not always have a choice about what kind of culture the organization should have. In our lily pond analogy, I have discussed how deeply rooted the fundamental assumptions of the culture may be. Therefore, leaders need to assume that in most cases they will need to work with the existing culture. This will require them to understand the elements of their existing culture and how it impacts any strategic decisions that might be made.

Before we leave the subject of organizational culture, it might be good to mention one more example of an individual that truly understood culture and its importance to the organization. This person was Ken Olsen, the former CEO of Digital Equipment Corporation.

DEC was started in 1957. This was well before the value shift that took place in Western societies and, as I have mentioned, influenced everything from the way we raise our children, to the way that computing is done. I do not know for sure what it was that influenced Ken to instill a culture that has become a standard in Western societies. I read, and heard it mentioned, that in addition to Ken's engineering talent, at a certain point in his history, he started reading and taking interest in a number of business management books. He has received great recognition for being a great entrepreneur and product visionary, but has never, in my estimation, received the credit that he is due for introducing a culture that continues to live on well beyond his lifetime.

In Chapter 6, I discussed elements of the DEC culture. At this point, when we are discussing what leaders should do to instill elements of the model that I have proposed in this book, it is good to mention Ken Olsen as a good role model for those who aspire to better understand culture and the role it plays in organizational success.

6. The strategy processes, as I have discussed, are powerful enablers for creating shared, desired, organizational results, for creating identification of the members of the organization with these desired results, and for enabling the interdependent way of working to achieve them. Leaders must understand how to accomplish these steps. In this book, I have

outlined ways that this can be done. The annual, strategic planning process provides an excellent opportunity to do this, but even more valuably, seeing the organization as an integrated whole with an interdependent way of working toward a desired, shared set of results should be an ongoing mindset for the organization. "How are we doing on our strategy and our long-term goals?" should be a question that is asked frequently by senior leaders.

7. We have argued that strategy is all about choices. Leaders of the organizational system must sometimes make difficult choices. In addition, they must clarify the choice that has been made. This, by itself, will in many cases bring other groups together in support of the selection. In an earlier section of the book, I used the example of the company that could not choose customer intimacy as its primary value discipline to illustrate what happens when functional heads decide priorities based upon their own leanings.

The importance of making strategic choices can also be highlighted by another of my consulting examples. With this particular client, I was asked to help them develop a strategic plan for the corporation. Prior to my executive planning session with them, I did a set of one-on-one interviews with the senior executive team. There are a number of tools that I use in these interviews. One is to ask the individuals that I am interviewing to rank order for me the following: customers, shareholders and employees. Which in her estimation would she rank number one, two and three in importance? Consistency, or not, between the answers of all the executives, reveals to me much about the company and its philosophy of success.

A second tool that I will often use is to have the senior executives individually rank order for me: time, cost and quality. Which do they consider to be the number one priority in the company? Again, this tells me much about how the company is positioning itself for success.

In the example that I am discussing, I used the latter tool with the senior executives, and later summarized my findings with the CEO of the company. My discussion with him went as follows:

"I met with each of your executives, and among other things, I asked them to rank order time, cost and quality. Which did they see as the number one priority for the company and why? The results were interesting," I noted. "There was general agreement that 'time' was the number one priority of the company, but they struggled to arrive at that answer. A number asked if they couldn't make both time and quality number one. Is it possible," I added, "that quality is too high a priority for you?" The CEO responded, "Pete, I have been wondering the same thing myself."

We see from the above example a company that had still not yet made a strategic choice. Whereas everyone discussed that "time" was their ultimate imperative, in practice, they had not yet delivered on this priority. The company was missing time-to-market advantages because it was focusing too much on the quality of the product when it was released to market. Our discussion helped the company refocus its strategy on getting products to market before competition and releasing products that were "good enough."

8. In addition to the steps that I have outlined, the organization as system also uses systems thinking to make better decisions and to more effectively solve problems. Leaders should both model this skill and develop it in the senior members of their organization. Research shows that senior leaders tend to be systems thinkers. Among other things, they tend to focus on the pattern, as opposed to getting buried in the intricate details. As individuals rise in an organization, this is a valuable skill for them to acquire.

I have used the Inquiry Mode Questionnaire (InQ)[3] in my consulting work and leadership development work at Santa Clara University, to sensitize clients and students to the need to adapt their communication techniques to suit the thinking style of the individual with whom they are interfacing. The InQ looks at how people process information and it stays away from personality measurements that might lead to defensiveness.

The InQ uses a set of 18 questions, each followed by five possible responses which the individual must force rank from five, which is most typical of the individual's style, through one, which is least typical of the individual's style. The questionnaire yields a score for each of the five thinking styles, described in InQ Educational Materials, 2001.

- *Synthesist* – people who focus their thinking on ideas, and find connections among things that other people see as having little or no relationship.
- *Idealist* – people who experience reality as the whole into which new data are assimilated, based on perceived similarities to things they already know.
- *Pragmatist* – people who perceive a world constantly changing and largely unpredictable, requiring a flexible "whatever works" approach to problem-solving.
- *Analyst* – people who see the world as structured, organized and predictable, and who believe there should be one best method for doing anything.
- *Realist* – people who are inductive, and whose mental models are derived chiefly from observation and their own experience.

The *Idealist* thinking style is closest to the systems thinker that I have described – one who sees the pattern, the "big picture," and is not excessively drawn in by the data. The *Synthesist* is also somewhat interesting to us. While it is a rare thinking style (out of a class of 20–30 students, I would usually see one, or no, *synthesists*), they tend to see everything connected. They also are the "Devil's Advocates" in the group. They will tend to see the opposite of everything, a trait that can irritate others in the group.

I have used the tool with a number of corporate teams. As mentioned, it is an excellent communication tool. People learn why it is that sometimes they see things differently than their boss, or others. For our purposes here, the tool can be used by senior leaders to assess what their thinking bias tends to be. The majority of people we have tested tend to be systems thinkers, i.e., *idealists*. But what if one is not an *idealist*? This is a question perhaps for another time, but it would still be beneficial to know that, for example, one's thinking bias is *analyst*. The individual can then be sensitive to his bias in interactions with others and in his own work.

An example of the power of thinking styles comes from one of my client experiences a few years ago. I had a senior IT executive who had asked me to conduct a management workshop for her team. As part of the workshop, I used the InQ tool. It was one of the first times I had used it outside of my university work. Some weeks after the workshop, the IT executive shared with me an experience she had had with the Chief Operating Officer (COO) of the company. She indicated that she had always had difficulty communicating with this individual, and having recently been exposed to the Thinking Styles assessment tool, she decided to try what she had learned on the COO. She told me that she had theorized that the COO was a synthesist; therefore, he would want to see all sides of an argument. She accordingly presented him two possible solutions to a problem they were discussing, instead of just one. She proceeded to tell me that it was the best call she had ever had with the COO.

I have just discussed what the strategic leader at the top of the organization should do. In this latter discussion, I repeated the major argument that strategic leaders can most effectively influence the organization as system, strategically and culturally. A number of chapters in this book have dealt with these latter subjects. It leaves, however, a very important topic for us to discuss here – namely, influence itself. In the book, I have dealt with the broader impact of influence on the wider organizational body. What remains is to deal with it on an interpersonal basis.

My original intent in the following section was to discuss leadership at the levels below the top of the organization. I believe, however, that senior leaders can also derive great benefit from the material that follows.

Developing the Skill of Influence

I believe it is fair to say that effective leaders, in general, have a strong ability to influence others. Two years ago, I conducted a series of seminars on influence skills for senior and middle managers. Generally misunderstood and unknown are the many ways one can be influential. In the following section, I will outline a number of these methods.

Influence Seminar Series

Figure 7.1 shows the content from my influence series.

Deliver a comprehensive, multi-faceted view of influence to include:

- Macro Versus Micro Influence
- Sales Techniques
- Marketing
- Thinking Styles
- Influence Styles
- Practical Influence Strategies
- Influence Without Authority
- Role of Relationships
- Role of Effective Communications

Figure 7.1 The Approach.

Space will not permit me to address the entire content of my seminars, but my intent is to summarize the key points from that series that will help senior individuals, and lower- and mid-level managers, to exert greater leadership in their organization. Again, my premise is that in order to become a stronger strategic leader, one of the best things you can do is to become more influential.

The techniques I will share with the reader come from my own practical experience and from a variety of disciplines. Let me start first with defining the difference between micro and macro influence. Micro influence is that between individuals. It is the most common form of influence. Micro influence techniques are especially important, for example, in selling ideas to a superior, or to someone higher in the chain of command.

Macro influence, on the other hand, is that achieved with the wider organization. Becoming knowledgeable in strategy and using it to influence the organization, is an example of macro influence.

Marketing

Marketing can be both a micro influence and a macro influence technique. There are many definitions of marketing. Classically, marketing is defined by the 4Ps – productizing, promotion, packaging and pricing. I have also heard it defined somewhere as a technique to "raise awareness of value." The following diagram has been very useful to me for defining marketing and for its practical applications.

The reader might recall that I used this diagram earlier to describe how a company might develop its competitive strategy. In a similar way, we could use it to develop a marketing strategy for the company's products. For our purposes, however, we could use this diagram as a micro influence tool to "raise awareness of one's value," i.e., to market oneself. In this latter case, one circle of the diagram would contain a person's unique skills, strengths and experiences. These would intersect certain organizational needs, in a way that differentiates the individual from competitive alternatives.

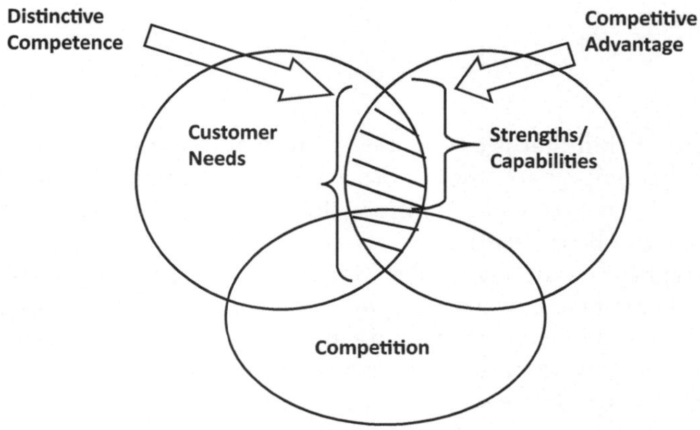

Figure 4.5 A Competitive Model

On one occasion, I used Figure 4.5 to seek a position at Santa Clara University. Previously, I had had an industrial career with two major computer companies. When the second company ran into serious financial difficulties, I took early retirement and started a strategy consultancy. A former partner at one of the large consulting firms had advised me to seek, in parallel with my consulting, a university role. Conversations with one of the university department heads subsequently led me to an opportunity with the group that offered continuing education to Silicon Valley individuals.

Using Figure 4.5, I completed the circle showing what I believed were my capabilities in a number of areas. These even included some training, course development and classroom education, but nothing like the competition I would face from other academics. Among my strengths, I needed to find something that uniquely addressed a problem that the university had. The break came in a conversation with the head of the department and his comment that their seminars were not being sold successfully. In turn, this led me to highlight my extensive marketing experience to help them better market their seminars – something, it turned out, no other academic could offer.

Let me discuss another way that an individual might use marketing as a macro influence technique to show their leadership in the corporation. The individual might, for example, introduce the Venn diagram we have just discussed to people in other functions and at other levels. The introduction might come with an invitation for them to work together to develop a competitive strategy for the corporation. Once completed, the suggestion might be made to share the results with a senior corporate executive. This is an example showing how a leader might influence a wider audience to adopt the thematic solution I have proposed in this book. In the example, a unique marketing diagram might be used to influence others in the company to work interdependently and to develop knowledge that will help the company be more competitive.

Sales

Next, let us look at a skill that is closely related to marketing – namely, sales. There is the mistaken impression that in order to be influential one must be a sales-type person. Shortly, we will look more closely at this argument and see that almost anyone can be influential.

I spent many years as a Salesman, Sales Manager, and even spent years as a Sales Training Manager in a very large corporation. What we teach salespeople is actually very basic. The heart of the training is repetition of the basics, as we put them into role-play scenarios in which they must perform the skills we have taught them. For our purposes, there are a few skills we can learn from sales that will help strategic leaders be more influential.

The first of these basic skills is called features/benefits. We teach salespeople not to focus so much on the features of the product or service that they are selling, but rather on the benefits of those products or services to the customer. We drill this skill into them repeatedly.

In one of my sales training classes, I would often play the role of the customer in an exercise in which the new salesperson would practice the features/benefits routine. In scenarios that I recall, we had the salesperson selling a new computer product to me. Frequently, the new salesperson would proceed to tell me how much more capacity the new computer had and how much faster it performed. After listening to this for a while, I would often reach behind me and take a baseball cap off my shelf and place it on my head. Across the brim of the hat, written in large capital letters, were the words **SO WHAT**. The point was that customers don't really care how fast or how large the computer is, we would tell the salesperson, he wanted to know what the computer could do for him.

The **SO WHAT** technique is a very simple one – yet, it is very powerful in communicating benefits to the customer. Individuals can learn this skill and apply it whenever they are trying to influence someone in the organization about an idea they have, or an action that might be taken by the company. In those situations, remember to develop a mindset that asks, "What is in it for the customer?"

Another technique we teach salespeople is that of "closing." Simply stated, this involves asking the customer a question that requires a "yes" or "no" response. It can be used in any situation in which an individual is seeking final approval of a product proposal, idea, or even resulting meeting actions. It is amazing to me how seldom we use this technique in our day-by-day occurrences, and yet, it is a very powerful technique.

Generally, the close is preceded by a summary of the benefits to the person or group we are trying to influence. An example of the closing statement might be, "Is there any reason we cannot proceed with this proposal?" At this point, silence is recommended on the part of the influencer, as the "yes" or "no" response is awaited. A "yes" response means that the person has done a good job. A "no" response tells the person that he has further work to do.

In addition to the features/benefits technique and the closing technique, there are a number of other things we teach new salespeople. One of them is how to handle objections. I won't go into the details of this process here, except to emphasize a portion of the skill that is extremely important to both salespeople and others that want to be influential, that is, the skill of listening. In my experience with salespeople, I have found that new salespeople tend to talk too much. As they advance and become better salespeople, they become better listeners. Later, I will talk about this skill of listening in more detail.

Thinking Styles

Earlier, I discussed the thinking styles work that we did at Santa Clara University. Here I would like to talk about how one can use their thinking style to influence others, and therefore become better leaders. How we think is not something that most of us spend much time analyzing. The power of an instrument to measure thinking styles, such as the InQ, is that we become aware of how we think and how it influences those we interact with.

In my class at the university, I will ask my students if, in influencing someone, it is more important to use one's own thinking style, or the thinking style of the person we are trying to influence. The answer is that in order to influence someone else we need to be sensitive to that other person's thinking style. We must put things into a framework that they personally favor. For example, a person that has a dominant analyst thinking style, in an interaction with a person that prefers to see the big picture and not a lot of data, must learn how to present his proposal or petition in a big picture format.

My thinking style shows me to be dominant in both the idealist, i.e., the systems thinking and big picture style, and the pragmatist style, which shows a bias for taking action. At times, I have struggled when interfacing with people who are dominant in the analyst thinking style. My tendency is generally to focus on things like purpose, long-term goals and patterns. I have had to learn to focus more on data, structure and logic when dealing with analysts.

"Positive Power and Influence"

Earlier, I indicated that I would question the mistaken impression that only salespeople can be influential. My thinking has been greatly influenced by a seminar I attended some years ago entitled "Positive Power and Influence."[4] This was an intensive, five-day event and analyzed one's personal, influence style. To accomplish this, they videotaped role-plays and later reviewed them in discussions of one's dominant style.

In the seminar, we were told that we would be looking at four different influence styles. These were as follows:

- Reward and Punishment
- Participation and Trust
- Common Vision
- Assertive Persuasion

Reward and punishment are used when one has the authority to act in this manner. We tend to see these styles in hierarchical organizations with strong professional management cultures. They are no longer as popular in Western societies.

Participation and trust is an influence style that we see in people who make us feel valued. In their communication with us, we come away feeling they are listening to us and are interested in us. They ask questions about us and listen actively and respectfully to the answers. Because of how they make us feel, we trust them, and are willing to be influenced by them as a result.

The participation and trust style of influence is a powerful way to get others to relate strongly to us. Unfortunately, we more often encounter people who spend almost their entire time telling us about them. People who want to become leaders in organizations should look seriously at this style of influence. It is not a difficult one to learn; rather, it just takes a mindset that values others and "wants to hear their story."

Another behavior used by those who practice participation and trust is the repetition of what they have heard the other party say, or of the emotion that they have experienced from the other person. Once again, this makes the other party feel that they have been heard, and therefore valued.

The common vision style of influence involves creating a favorable picture of the future. This type of person draws a compelling vision of the future that both excites us and compels us to join her in pursuing. At some point in our lives, most of us have experienced this influence style. It could have been from a teacher, painting a picture of success that would come from our hard, learning work. Alternatively, we might have experienced this style from a boss, or top executive, who envisioned for us the success that would come from a new action the company had just taken.

The assertive persuasion person uses logic and data to make his argument. He carefully constructs these to lead others to a certain conclusion. Syllogistic thinking, for example, might be a technique this person uses.

The reader, perhaps, has already correlated some of the foregoing influence styles to our discussions about thinking styles. We can see, for example, that the person whose dominant thinking style deals with systems thinking and the big picture might use common vision to influence others. It might also be easy to see that the analyst thinking style person would employ assertive persuasion to influence others. Regardless, the purpose of this discussion about my attendance at the "positive power and influence" seminar has been simply to demonstrate that anyone can be influential. Whether they adopt one of the styles from the seminar, or adopt another influence idea that I have mentioned, they have many ways they can use to become influential.

Robert Cialdini

One of my favorite authors on the subject of influence is Robert Cialdini, a professor at Arizona State University. In fact, his book, entitled *Influence*,[5] is a textbook used by many universities. I use one of his 60-minute videos in my seminars at the university and in other public events. In the video he details six principles of "ethical influence." The principle I like best is that of reciprocation. Robert says that this involves being the first to give service, information or concessions. In other words, you lead by giving the other person one of the latter, and society's expectation, as Dr. Cialdini mentions, is that they will reciprocate and give you something in return.

Closely related to the principle of reciprocation is a mindset that focuses on the success of another person, or another group. Some years ago, I took a new management position at Digital Equipment Corporation. One of my first acts as a manager has always been to get to know my people. Generally, this involves an interview with each individual very soon after I have taken my new position. I remember vividly one individual from that time. He was somewhat older than I and met with me for us to get to know one another. I will never forget his comment to me as he came in. In the sincerest manner, he said, "Pete, I want to do everything I can to help you and the group be successful." I was deeply touched by Bert's comments, and indeed, he went on to live by this message. It was not just words. Subsequently, I trusted Bert and was greatly influenced by him. *It's a lesson for all of us; cultivate and communicate a mindset that says to others that you want to help them be successful. In return, you will become more influential.*

The Role of Relationships

In our next two sections, I will talk about the role of relationships and the role of effective communication in becoming more influential. Let us begin by talking about the role of relationships. We generally assume that relationships are important if we want to influence another individual or another group. There are many books written about relationships. Our purpose here is to highlight some unique aspects of relationship building that will help us be more influential.

In influencing others, one of the most important things we can convey to them is that we are credible. We can define "credible" as the state of being both competent and trustworthy. Being competent means that people see us as having the requisite knowledge and skills. Being seen as trustworthy is much more complex. It might mean that people can depend upon us; it can also mean that we do not cheat or lie.

We have discussed the importance of listening before. The act of listening is also important in forming relationships with others. This is brilliantly stated in the following quote by the esteemed psychologist, Carl Rogers.

> So, as you can readily see from what I have said thus far, a creative, active, sensitive, accurate, empathic, nonjudgmental listening is for me terribly important in a relationship.[6]

I will often ask my students, "When, if ever, have you ever heard the act of listening described with so many adjectives?" I will then relate to them that Carl Rogers literally uses each adjective to describe the potential power of listening.

Another Carl Rogers quote that I love, and one that is applicable for those who wish to become leaders, is the following.

> In our work with students it's the quality of our relationship with them, not the content we teach, that is the most significant element determining our effectiveness.[7]

While Carl Rogers is talking about teachers, for us it highlights once again the importance of relationships in becoming a leader. Without a strong relationship, people will be less likely to want to be led by you.

The Role of Effective Communications

As with relationship building, there have been many books written about effective communications. In this next discussion, I would like to focus on a few key communication skills from my own practical experience.

We have already discussed the power of listening as an aid to effective relationship building. We have also discussed its role in the Participation and Trust style of influence. Listening, coupled with strong questioning techniques, can be a powerful formula for not only building relationships, but also discerning the needs of those we seek to please. The formula basically consists of asking good, open-ended questions, and then listening effectively to the responses.

In both my sales work and consulting work, I have had to teach many individuals how to do effective questioning. In both sales and consulting, it is very important to understand in-depth the needs of the customer. From a determination of those needs, it is much easier to go to a product or solution that addresses those needs and produces a sale.

When questioning about needs, it is important to ask open-ended questions. These are questions that do not require a yes or no response, but rather, get the other party speaking, and hopefully, providing valuable information. As I mentioned before, in these interactive sessions with a customer or client, it is important to try to put oneself in the customer's shoes and to understand not only the need of the customer, but also very importantly, the value of satisfying that need for the customer.

I can remember well one experience I had when coaching an IT individual on how to do this type of questioning. On this occasion, the subject individual and I met before making a call on one of his internal clients. We discussed that our objective was to determine the high-level needs of this client. We would use the questioning techniques that he and I had previously discussed in order to accomplish this.

Before leaving for the client's office, the IT person related that he was currently working on a project for this client that involved furnishing them a specialized report. He mentioned that they were having difficulty with the client, because she kept changing her mind on the details of the report. I restated our objective to give him an opportunity to practice the questioning technique that we had discussed, but if we had the opportunity, we would explore the report issue.

Arriving at the client's office, we proceeded to ask her general, high-level, business questions, such as, "What is the mission of your group? How are you measured? How would you define success? Etc." The client was very helpful and we gathered a large amount of information about what her group did and how they could achieve success.

Eventually sensing an opportunity, I remarked to the client that I was aware that IT was working on a report for them. "Could she please tell me what value this report would provide her," I asked. She proceeded to tell me that the report was to be used in order to provide the doctors they served a comparison of two different types of services that they might be asked to deliver. Totals at the bottom of the report would tell them how much they would earn from each of these alternatives. Apparently, the doctors felt strongly that the totals would show that they stood to lose if they accepted a new service that had been proposed. The client, however, hoped to show the doctors that this difference did not exist.

At this point, I turned to the IT person and saw that he looked somewhat pale and bothered. It turns out that the disagreement over the client's report dealt with IT having omitted the totals from the report. They had left out the most important part of the report, because they had never asked, "What will you use this report for? What value will it provide you?"

The example I have just related is intended to convey to the prospective leader how important it is for them to understand in-depth the needs of those they are trying to influence. I have stated that the right kind of questioning is a powerful technique for getting at those needs. My example goes further, however, to illustrate the further benefit of what we call in sales, the "implication question." The implication question might have been used by our IT person to determine the value that the client would have hoped to receive from the report.

Leadership Below the Top

In my introductory book section on the "intended audience," I stated that I would later address ways that individuals lower in the organization can provide leadership to the overall corporation. Indeed, a contemporary belief is that "leadership can come from anywhere;" it doesn't just have to come from someone at the top of the corporation. *While this is a fair statement, I have seen little or no practical examples of how this type of leadership might be developed.* In this section, I hope to address this absence.

We might start by asking how the leadership below the executive level differs from the leadership at the top. I have stated that leadership at the top has the ability to move the "whole" of the organization, and can effectively do this, strategically and culturally. Leaders lower in the organization do not have that capability or vantage point. They are, however, part of the formula, as I have stated, that can unleash their creative talents and energy in support of the success of the "whole." This latter capability is enhanced, as I have discussed, with an organizational culture that empowers and trusts them.

Getting more specific, we can look at a number of ways that people lower in the organization can "lead." They can, for example, submit ideas. They also can submit observations about how the strategy is working or not. And they can certainly lead by drawing others in their group and other groups to work together for the good of the "whole." *I will submit that each of these and other examples depend on the ability of the person at lower levels in the organization to influence someone.* In the previous section, I outlined many generic skills that the individual can employ to make the latter happen. Let us look here at some other ideas tied more directly to the main theme of this book.

If we start with the model that I have proposed in this book, we could say that one way for individuals lower in the organization to create influence is by becoming more knowledgeable about business strategy – especially its processes, and also, organizational culture. As I have already indicated, there is a dearth of good strategy and cultural knowledge at senior levels of corporations. By becoming more knowledgeable on these subjects, individuals and mid-level managers can utilize their unique knowledge to advance the intellectual assets of the company.

Earlier, I discussed how senior leaders can develop strategic capability in their corporation by reading good strategic material and discussing relevant content in staff meetings and other forums. I mentioned that good sources were the *Harvard Business Review*, *Sloan Management Review*, and the newsletters that come from the consulting firms of McKinsey and Booz and Company. Individuals at levels below the executive offices can also derive significant benefit by reading good strategic material and circulating relevant articles to others in the organization. The secret is to circulate articles that are relevant to the organization. For example, it might be an article that addresses a business need that the corporation is currently struggling with. Emerging technologies are also an excellent source of material. They generally represent areas that can be viewed as either opportunities or threats for a company, and as such, are generally of great interest to senior audiences.

In my years at IBM, I learned the value of educating senior executives on emerging technologies. During my subsequent years at Digital Equipment Corporation, I once applied this knowledge to educate a group of senior executives about artificial intelligence (AI). This was one of the many times that AI has promised significant benefits to corporations and others. Articles about AI appeared prominently on the cover of media, such as the *Wall Street Journal* and *Business Week*. I had learned that in all probability when an emerging technology makes the headlines, senior business executives would want to understand this new technology and take advantage of what it had to offer.

I was amazed at the sizable audience that came to a one-day seminar on AI. In fact, we turned away 64 people because we did not have enough room for them. In the audience were 15 corporate presidents and other senior leaders that had come to understand AI and what it could do for their company. Those individuals and managers that want to be leaders in their organization can take a clue from my experience. Educating senior executives on emerging technologies is an excellent way for you to demonstrate leadership. Whether you do it in a classroom, or by circulating a relevant article, it will be greatly appreciated by those whose knowledge you have enhanced.

Some corporations have housed individuals with specialized knowledge in internal consulting organizations. Digital Equipment Corporation, for example, had such an internal resource. Instead of calling upon external consultants in all cases, internal resources were available that had not only certain requisite knowledge, but also an excellent working knowledge of the company and how it worked.

Another way that employees at lower levels in the organization can provide leadership is by having their group serve as a pilot for the corporation. An individual in a functional, corporate group might, for example, offer their function to test the model I have introduced in this book. As I have indicated previously, the latter model can work either at a group level, or at a corporate level. In a very large corporation, piloting the model at a group level would be an excellent way to prove its worth and to provide needed learning for subsequent implementation at wider levels in the corporation.

Closely related to the pilot idea is the idea of using the strategy processes that I have discussed in this book to influence the corporate strategy. This is another way for individuals and groups to provide leadership to the wider corporation. An example of this is a university with whom I consulted. In this case, a functional group in the university was having difficulties developing its own strategic plan because of the lack of an overall, university, strategic plan. My bold recommendation to the functional group was that they develop a strategic plan for the university. I proceeded to tell them that for their purposes, the most important part of this university strategic plan would be the long-term goals. These would serve as the shared results that all the functions in the university needed to know in order to determine how they would best contribute to their achievement.

The functional group proceeded to develop university long-term goals. Using principles that I have articulated about goals and how best to develop them, the group ended up with a set of goals that allowed them to continue with the development of their own strategic plan. Perhaps more importantly, when they presented this plan to university executives, they were able to favorably influence the conduct of the university strategic plan. The message to the university executives was simple: "We see ourselves as a resource and as a means to help you achieve your university goals. We trust that the goals that we have assumed for you reflect credibly on goals that you would have established for yourself."

The foregoing example is a powerful way for groups to provide leadership to their corporation. I have seen it work many times in the absence of strong strategic capability at the executive level. Senior executives generally welcome this intervention and I believe the reader will see my example as a good way to highlight how a group might gain visibility with their senior executives. Being seen as a leader in the important area of strategy might subsequently provide the group further opportunities to provide value to the overall corporation.

I also include this example to reinforce one significant aspect of the model that I have proposed in this book. Earlier, I mentioned that workers would derive great benefit from seeing how their work contributed to the good of the "whole;" it would provide them nobility of purpose. *Never, however, did I expect to hear the following comments from one of the individuals at the conclusion of my work with them. Turning to me, he said, "Pete, I never realized how the work that I did connected with the overall good of the university. I saw my work as technical, and while important, I never connected it in this manner before. It makes me proud of what we do."*

We have not yet discussed how people below the top can use the knowledge of culture to exhibit strong leadership in a corporation. In several client organizations with whom I have consulted, there has been a noticeable conflict between the corporate culture and the culture of the group with whom I was working. In the latter case, I have often suggested to my client that having a subculture different from the parent culture is not an unworkable problem. To make my point, I have used the successful examples of Lockheed and IBM. Lockheed, for example, developed their SR 71 spy plane in a skunk works whose culture was significantly more empowered than that of the parent company. Likewise, IBM developed its first personal computer similarly in a skunk works at a time when IBM's parent culture was strongly one of professional management.

My subsequent work with clients has usually involved showing them how differences in culture can work to their advantage. I have learned that understanding the differences between the parent culture and the subculture – especially the strong friction points – is essential. It is also important to be able to communicate about these differences with the parent. Doing the latter is an excellent way to exhibit leadership for the intermediate-level manager.

This concludes my chapter on "Leadership of the Organization as System." In this chapter, I have attempted to support my argument that leadership of the organizational system is different from traditional leadership – especially at the top of the organization. Leadership at the top involves knowledge of the strategy processes and culture, and the use of them, to move the organizational system as a whole, to some desired destination. It also involves leadership of the interactions that occur between individuals and groups in the company, as part of these processes.

This chapter has also included a discussion of leadership below the executive level. As I mentioned earlier, there is much said about people at all levels of the organization being leaders. Sadly, very little is written about how they achieve this status. I have argued that leaders need to be influential. As a result, I have taken the opportunity in this chapter to discuss detailed, practical ways that individuals, at both the top of the organization and below, can become more influential.

References

1. Marco Iansiti, "Real World R&D: Jumping the Product Generation Gap," *Harvard Business Review*, May–June 1993.
2. Webster Robinson, *Harvard Business Review*, April 1925.
3. Authors: A. Harrison, R. Bramson, S. Bramson, N. Parlette. The InQ is a proprietary assessment instrument, developed and marketed by InQ Materials, LLC, located in Palouse, WA, USA.
4. The company was founded by Kevin Munro, running its first Positive Power and Influence Program in 1983. It continues to be the property of Chartwell Learning & Development.
5. Robert Cialdini, *Influence* (Quill Publications, 1984).
6. Carl R. Rogers, *A Way of Being* (Houghton Mifflin Company, 1980).
7. Ibid.

8 Getting Started

Introduction

In the introduction to this book, I mentioned that diverse audiences might find individual chapters of interest to them. Individuals interested in General Systems Theory, for example, will find in Chapter 1 a summary of its basics expressed by some of the great world masters. In Chapter 7, I also offer individuals wanting to become leaders in their organization unique, practical tips for accomplishing this. For the persons below the top levels of their organization, I especially offer my unique perspective on perhaps the most significant leadership skill – namely, the skill of "influence."

In this book, however, the main theme has dealt with going beyond interest in individual subjects, such as systems theory and leadership, and proposing a comprehensive solution that I believe will enhance corporate performance. Given a desire to explore this latter model, how would a company proceed? Are there good reasons for the company to start with only a portion of it? For example, the company may want to start slowly and try simple random ideas that I have suggested. Alternatively, the company may feel strong overall, but would like to become stronger in certain areas. If so, what portions of the model that we have discussed would be most beneficial for these kinds of organizations?

To answer the foregoing questions, I would like to suggest that many organizations could benefit from enhancement of the strategy processes. As I have hopefully illustrated, there is much that companies could gain from having more effective strategy creation and execution processes. Let us look further at this option.

As I indicated in our section on strategy, there is tremendous confusion about strategy. I have tried to simplify it in order that organizations can take greater advantage of its potential. Companies can gain a great deal by reviewing again my section on strategy and beginning to apply those principles and ideas that are relevant for their organization. They may also wish to review again the suggestions I made for those companies that wish to embed greater strategic capability into their organization.

I made a special point that strategy execution in most companies has been a tragic failure. A company can significantly improve its execution of strategic initiatives by reviewing the section on strategy execution and applying what they learn from it to their organization. Even a slight improvement may provide the organization a competitive advantage.

I believe I need to say very little additional about the strategy processes. I feel confident that almost any organization, of any size or industry makeup, can profit from developing greater strategic capability and processes. There is large untapped potential here for the companies that wish to pursue these.

Assuming one is still undecided about how to proceed, are there other things to consider? I believe a good next step for an organization is an assessment of its culture. If it perceives that it has a strong, top-down, control culture, the interdependent way of working that I have described will be more of a challenge. The latter requires a collaborative culture that empowers and trusts people. It is the "entrepreneurial" type culture that I described in the section on culture. If one does not have this latter type of culture, is there nothing that can be done?

Recent change efforts have recognized that while wholesale cultural change is very difficult, it is possible to change certain cultural behaviors. Earlier, in my chapter on organizational culture, I described a company that successfully accomplished this (see "The Learning Culture"). The strategy processes and associated tools provide us a means to do something similar. Let me elaborate.

The strategy process that I recommended in Chapter 4 involved senior stakeholders coming together to debate the future of the company. For some companies, this might be a very different way to do strategic planning. In this case, it will require great trust on the part of senior leaders who might fear loss of control with the new process. Let's assume, however, that a decision is made to give the collaborative process a try. What is likely to happen as a result?

- The executive planning meeting is a disaster. The loss of control that was feared actually happened and nothing was accomplished.
- The executive planning meeting was a success. There were some uncomfortable moments with everyone trying to voice their opinions, but overall the resulting plan was creative and looks very solid. And people seemed sincerely to be very excited about the results.

Obviously, a successful meeting would be a greater enabler of change. Going forward, perhaps the senior leaders would see now the power of engaging a talented group of individuals and trusting them with the future of the company.

An organization with the control type culture can also benefit from the ideas that I have expressed in the sections on the strategy processes. In fact, I believe that adopting some of these ideas will provide them even greater control and better performance. Improving strategy execution will especially serve as a means to accomplishing the latter.

Next, let us discuss the organization that perceives that it has an empowering type culture and wishes to pursue some of the ideas in this book. Where should they focus and how should they start? As with the control type culture,

I believe the best place to start would be the strategy processes. By focusing on the strategy creation process and the successful execution of the strategy that has been created, the company's interdependent way of working will be further enhanced. Attention should also be paid to the section on leadership of the organizational system. As the reader may recall, in the latter section I have stressed the importance of leadership of the organizational interactions. This new form of leadership, coupled with strong strategy processes that enable people working together for the good of the overall organization, will produce greater organizational performance.

Dealing with Change

Let us discuss now some of the obstacles that an organization might encounter as they attempt to put some of the ideas in this book into action. Perhaps the strongest obstacle will be to overcome a very long history. As I have indicated, for almost the past 400 years, the world has been strongly influenced by the Newtonian/Descartes way of thinking. The effect of this thinking on organizations has been to put the emphasis on the parts of the organization, as opposed to the whole. Our emphasis in the Western culture on the individual has also contributed to a style of thinking that is contrary to the interdependent way of working that I have stressed in this book.

Another obstacle is the strong identification of individuals with their functional organization. Earlier I stated that individuals see themselves strongly as salespeople or engineers, for example.

Yet another obstacle is the fear that individuals and groups will lose something from the changes that are proposed in the organization. An allegorical story might highlight the strength of this fear. I don't remember where I first heard it related. It is a story that I have often told when dealing with change management issues.

There were two candy stores across the street from one another. On the surface, they appeared to have very similar merchandise and to charge comparable prices. What was surprising was the quantity of people that frequented these two stores. In the one case, people often stood in line outside in order to purchase their candy. On the other hand, the other store was frequently empty of customers.

A researcher observed these two different customer patterns and finally asked the worker at the busy candy store the following question:

> I have been watching your two candy stores for some time and have noticed that you are always very busy and your competitor across the street generally has very few customers. At the same time, I cannot see any difference between you and your competitor in the quality of your product, or the prices that you charge. What accounts for the profound differences in the number of customers that frequent your stores?

The response of the candy store attendant was as follows.

> If you watch very carefully the attendant across the street, you will see that she selects a certain amount of candy, puts it on the scale, and then, removes a portion of it. On the other hand, if you watch me, you will see that I select a portion of candy, place it on the scale, and then, add another small portion.

The point of the story is that as long as individuals perceive that something is being taken away from them, they will always react negatively. On the other hand, if they perceive that something is being added to them, they will react positively. I advise clients, therefore, that a major way to get individuals to accept any organizational change is by presenting it as a positive change for them.

There are obviously other change management issues and remedies that we could discuss. Many books have already been written that deal with these subjects, but perhaps I could summarize a few key thoughts of my own. The following is abstracted from my report to a client, a senior management team. In the following example, the senior team had done a brilliant job of developing a new, integrated, business strategy for the company. What appeared to me to be missing, however, were the things that destroy many brilliant, future visions – the people, culture and change management considerations. Here are my comments to them, along with associated recommendations.

Does the change management process need to start with the executive team?

> If the organization proceeds toward an integrated vision, this will have profound effects on the work to be performed, and very likely, the resulting organizational structure. Is the senior team prepared for this eventuality? How will the cross-functional issues be addressed? Will people feel threatened, if they perceive that the proposed changes will result in a loss of power for them? Are people prepared to sacrifice self-interests, if necessary, for the good of the organization? Effective strategy is all about making choices. As a result, functional heads that make up the top management group each stand to gain or lose from the choices that are made. Is the teamwork and communications at the senior levels strong enough to deal effectively with these challenges?
>
> We need to continue to extend our dialogue with the senior team. Is this wider audience truly committed to the integrated vision? And does the wider audience understand and buy into our proposed change management process? Or, more likely, do they think that change management is confined to very narrow boundaries, such as staffing plans and communications issues?
>
> **Recommendation:** Prior to unveiling the entire change management process, we need to prepare senior management for the eventualities of a fully-integrated strategic vision. In reality, the change management process needs to start with them, as we work together to define the integrated vision and its impact on them and their people. We also need to expand our contact with the members of the executive team as soon as possible.

One-on-one meetings with this audience, in which we pursue the people and change management issues, as well as the broader strategic execution issues, should be conducted.

The other recommendation in my report was to conduct one-on-one meetings with members of the executive team and other stakeholders. I include here the purpose of these interviews, as well as the actual questions, in order to provide the interested reader practical, tested, content that they may be able to use in their own change management efforts.

The purpose of the interviews was to inquire about people and change management types of issues and to determine the organization's readiness for change. Other objectives were as follows:

- Begin to bring the executive team on board with the overall change management process that needs to be put in place if the initiatives are to succeed.
- Surface any assumptions – conscious or unconscious – that might inhibit strategic success.
- Validate the preliminary observations in this report and explore possible solutions to remaining issues.
- Understand better the strategic efforts in their respective area as a first step toward understanding how best to integrate the strategic initiatives and to facilitate the associated change.

Following are the actual questions I used in the executive interviews:

- "What are the current strategic initiatives that your group is working on?"
- "How will they benefit your group? The organization as a whole?"
- "How would you assess the corporation's readiness for change? Your group's readiness for change? Do your people understand the need for change? How will you get your people to buy into the required changes?"
- "What are your thoughts on integrating the corporate initiatives, and creating in the process a new corporation? How would you describe this new end-state? What are the inhibitors to this happening? What new, empowered role could your people play in this new end-state?"
- "What effect, if any, will the corporate culture have on your initiatives and the integrated end-state that you described?"
- "How will your initiatives and/or the new corporate end-state affect the work to be performed? What impact will this have on your people? How will you make this a positive experience for them?"
- "What are the cross-functional issues in achieving an integrated vision?"
- "Do you anticipate any structural changes as a result of either your initiatives or the integrated initiatives? How will you deal with these?"

Returning to our earlier objections, how do we deal with the deeply-rooted silos, the products of long, established thinking? The foregoing example gives us some ideas, but I would be remiss if I oversimplified the solution. Change is difficult and it is hard work. As I mentioned in the Introduction to this book, the reality is that most companies, despite significant breakthroughs in so many industrial areas, continue to operate in organizational silos. I believe, however, that the new strategic leader, using the ideas I have proposed in this book, has a fresh way to break down the silos and to subsequently enhance organizational performance. Using the power of strategy processes as I have outlined to accomplish this, is to the best of my knowledge, an approach that has not been previously tried. Maybe the time has come to "give it a shot."

Postscript

While writing this book, it has been impossible to ignore the crisis that is facing our world. The pandemic has certainly touched all of us, and in the United States, the racial issues have complicated lives even more. We long for a solution that would bring us all together, across major divisions, to work together to solve these problems.

Naïvely perhaps, I reflect upon the model I have presented in this book as a possible solution. After all, I have argued that my model would bring people together across organizational divisions, to work for the greater good of the whole. In theory, at least, it should work for the United States, as well as for any corporation, university or nonprofit. But then reality sets in and I remember my experience trying to bring the state of Texas together with the business community and the academic system. It never got off the ground, because it was too complex, bureaucratic and there were too many self-interests. What makes me think my model could work for the greater U.S. system of government?

But what if, for starters, we could take a portion of my model? What if we could get a representative body of government officials to agree on a set of values that underlie what we stand for, and a set of desired U.S. goals over the next three to five years? That doesn't sound impossible to me. There are plenty of historical documents to draw upon for the values, and the goal development could come from the process I have recommended in Chapter 4 of this book. After all, our politicians don't seem to disagree on these items as much as they disagree on the means to achieve them. Party ideology, self-interests and other things stand in the way of agreement on what is best for the country.

If we could get a central government group to agree on goals and values, is there a way then to engage the "will of the people" to help us select the most effective means? For example, if this government group developed a menu of means to achieve the desired goals, could the people vote on the best ones?

It is late at night after working long hours on my book, so I think I will stop. Maybe someone can pick up where I left off. It still sounds like an unbelievable challenge to use the model from my book to solve a problem of such tremendous complexity. After all, others more gifted than I have tried and left behind only their theories on what right government might look like. During my leisure moments over the past several months, for example, I have read

Plato's Republic, and Thomas More's Utopia, in an effort to better understand the possibilities with our current governance structure.

Imagine a government that has agreed upon a set of values, a set of desired long-term results, and secured the "will of the people" on the best way to achieve these results. Perhaps our traditional government would now step in to operationalize the "will of the people." Of course, they need to work together to accomplish this, and maybe that is what they should have been doing right along.

Appendix: Sample Executive Planning Agenda

8:00 A.M.	Introduction Welcome Purpose of the Workshop Ground Rules Review the Agenda Expectations of the Attendees
9:00 A.M.	Environmental Analysis/Internal Assessment Discussion List the major conclusions from the pre-workshop analysis. Which of these, if any, may have a major impact on the strategic plan, and therefore, need to be discussed in the workshop? Where do they best fit on the agenda?
10:30 A.M.	Mission Does our current mission statement adequately capture the purpose of why we exist? Does our mission statement tell us what business we are in and clearly capture our strategic identity? (If it needs work, how do we best handle this off-line?)
11:30 A.M.	Vision As a group, envision the desired future state of the company. For our purposes, dream and assume that everything is possible. Later, we will convert these to realistic organizational goals.
1:00 P.M.	Goals Develop long-term, desired results (goals) for the company. Use the timeframe of the strategic plan. Use the criteria from this book.
4:00 P.M.	Finalize Goals Using the goal criteria from this book, develop a final list of organizational goals. These should be limited in number and adequately express the desired future state of the company. Reception and Dinner

Day 2

8:00 A.M. Review Day 1.
(Modify Day 2 agenda if necessary.)

9:00 A.M. Strategies

For each goal, develop a comprehensive means to achieve it. This should be a free-flowing exercise, capturing the creative inputs of all the participants. Brainstorming rules are appropriate.

An alternative approach – either in combination with the preceding method, or independently – is to address the major strategy categories. The latter, for example, would develop strategies in areas such as: product, competition, sales and marketing, distribution/logistics and operations. Again, it needs to be kept in mind that these strategies are means to achieve the goals that have been developed – not separate actions that the company will take.

It is also important to remind the workshop participants that the functional heads should, after the workshop, develop a plan for their respective area that examines their contribution to the corporate goals. In general, therefore, the executive team should select the strategy development method that balances the foregoing considerations. In the spirit of this book, it would also be beneficial to discuss those strategy categories that will include the majority of participants and lead them to work interdependently.

2:00 P.M. Prioritize Strategies

Before prioritizing the strategies, develop a list of criteria that will be used. An example is: contribution to the goal, cost, time to implement, risk, cultural fit, etc.

Several prioritization schemes are possible. Doing this exercise in the workshop helps the participants reach closure, but it should not substitute for a more analytical prioritization after the workshop, if needed.

4:00 P.M. Next Steps

Decide and list what remains to be done on the strategic plan. Also, decide how the remaining work will be accomplished. Assigning accountability for major steps is suggested.

Close

About the Author

Pete DeLisi claims that his interest in systems thinking stems from his long and eclectic career. It started with an undergraduate degree in chemistry from the University of Detroit. Upon graduation, he was commissioned as a Second Lieutenant in the Air Force and sent to the University of Wisconsin to attend an 18-month program in meteorology. This was followed by a six-year career as an Air Force meteorologist. Leaving the Air Force, he joined IBM to sell computers. During the years at IBM, Pete also did part-time graduate studies in both philosophy and psychology. Later, he was recruited by Digital Equipment Corporation (DEC). During the years at DEC, he met Ed Schein from the MIT Sloan School, and developed a love for organizational psychology. He later co-authored a book with Ed entitled, *DEC is Dead, Long Live DEC*. Pete served with DEC in a variety of senior management roles, and when they later ran into competitive difficulties, Pete left and started Organizational Synergies, a strategy consulting firm in Fremont, California. In parallel, he joined the faculty at Santa Clara University as Academic Dean of the IT Leadership Program. Now with his professional doors still open, he is enjoying writing and spending time with family.

Index

Note: Page numbers in *italics* indicate figures and in **bold** indicate tables on the corresponding pages.